THE GOSPELS *Behind*

THE GOSPELS *Behind* THE GOSPELS

Robert M. Price

PITCHSTONE PUBLISHING
DURHAM, NORTH CAROLINA

Pitchstone Publishing
www.pitchstonebooks.com

Library of Congress Cataloging-in-Publication Data

Names: Price, Robert M., 1954- author.
Title: The gospels behind the gospels / Robert M. Price.
Description: Durham, North Carolina : Pitchstone Publishing, [2023] |
   Includes bibliographical references. | Summary: "What if we have been
   missing a whole stage of how the canonical gospels came to be? What if
   there were a whole raft of prior Jesus narratives, the fragmentary
   vestiges of which now appear in Matthew, Mark, Luke, and John? This
   would explain why these gospels seem over-crowded with incompatible
   understandings of Jesus ("Christologies")? In The Gospels Behind the
   Gospels, innovative biblical scholar Robert M. Price attempts to
   reassemble the puzzle pieces, disclosing several earlier gospels of
   communities who imagined Jesus as the predicted return of the prophet
   Elijah, the Samaritan Taheb (a second Moses), a resurrected John the
   Baptist, a theophany of Yahweh, a Gnostic Revealer, a Zealot
   revolutionary, etc. As these various sects shrank and collapsed, their
   remaining followers would have come together, just as modern churches
   and denominations seek to survive by merging and consolidating. Our
   canonical gospels might be the result. Similarly, Price explores the
   possibility that Paul, Apollos, Cephas, and Christ were originally
   figureheads of rival sects who eventually merged in much the same way.
   You will never read the gospels the same way again!"— Provided by
   publisher.
Identifiers: LCCN 2022044002 (print) | LCCN 2022044003 (ebook) | ISBN
   9781634312387 (paperback) | ISBN 9781634312394 (ebook)
Subjects: LCSH: Bible. Gospels—Criticism, interpretation, etc.
Classification: LCC BS2555.52 .P746 2023 (print) | LCC BS2555.52 (ebook)
   | DDC 226/.06—dc23/eng/20221129
LC record available at https://lccn.loc.gov/2022044002
LC ebook record available at https://lccn.loc.gov/2022044003

Cover design by Qarol Price

*Dedicated to Darrin Griffin
with profound gratitude*

"If I could discover just one of those things . . .
I wouldn't care if they did say I was crazy!"

Dr. Henry Frankenstein

CONTENTS

INTRODUCTION

The Stereoscope

When you were a youngster did you play with the astonishing Viewmaster toy? It enabled you to behold photos in what at least *looked* like three-dimensional perspective. I still have mine, all these centuries later. (I wonder if my old pals Noah and Arphaxad still have theirs?) My favorites were the discs containing scenes from the twin TV series *Batman* and *The Green Hornet*, something that will hardly surprise you if you know me beyond the page! Anyway, the Viewmaster was what had earlier been called a stereoscope. It superimposed one image over another in such a way that you thought you were *there*, seeing the real thing. Well, I have come to suspect that when we read the New Testament gospels we are, in a manner of speaking, viewing their subject, Jesus Christ, stereoscopically. The image we receive of him, our hero, looks impressively real. But I suspect we are being "taken in," as literature takes us in, charming us into thinking we are seeing reality when in fact we are marveling at an artificial composite of superimposed images, neither of which by itself would look as it now appears to us.

What you are (I hope!) about to read is an exercise in speculative New Testament Christology. This approach is different from *theological* Christology, which seeks to formulate a theoretical doctrine normative for the belief of Christians. What I am attempting is to set forth a thought experiment in breaking down the gospel Jesus epic(s) into the component parts. The goal is nothing new, though I am bold to think that my method and result are innovative. There are many books on New Testament or gospel Christologies. Their authors are engaged in *descriptive*, not *prescriptive* exegesis. In other words, they are not trying to tell us what to believe, but rather what the biblical authors seem to have believed. Of course, to the disappointment of the theologians, neither the Bible as a whole nor any document within it sets forth a systematic theology, or theological system. Any system of biblical theology (or ethics for that matter) must be based on inference, and many very different inferences are possible.

The discipline of Biblical Theology appeared in the eighteenth-nineteenth centuries with prodigious tomes by Johann Salomo Semler, Johann Philipp Gabler, Johann Gottfried Eichhorn, Willibald Beyschlag, and others. It was a reaction against Lutheran (and other) theology which was essentially a series of expositions of creedal dogma employing scripture as a fund of proof-texts. In this way, Protestant theologians had retreated from Martin Luther's bold dictum that the Christian must first establish the teaching of the Bible, letting the chips fall where they may. Luther saw the situation as precisely analogous to that of King Josiah in 2 Kings, flabbergasted at the rediscovery of the Book of the Covenant (apparently some version of Deuteronomy). As his advisors read him the stipulations of the forgotten scripture, the king listened beneath a darkening cloud of doom and disbelief. If God had really wanted things done as this document commanded, then Judah must be in big trouble! So Josiah quickly launched a Cromwell-like program of sweeping religious and social reforms. Likewise, Luther sought to purify German Christianity from the unbiblical distortions, abuses, and corruptions (as he viewed them) including the sale of indulgences, papistical domination, the belief in Purgatory, and the virtual worship of Christian saints. But outsiders might well have found themselves unable to tell much difference between brand-new Lutheranism and old-time Catholicism. Many still can't.

Lutheran Protestantism demanded scriptural precedence over doctrinal creeds, but they quickly framed their own inflexible creed, the Augsburg Confession. It was difficult to think outside the creedal box. It seemed self-evident to them that the teaching of the Confession was at one with that of the Bible. But the centuries-later pioneers of the Biblical Theology Movement, weren't so sure. They braced themselves to stow their inherited dogma on the shelf (a "temporary willing suspension of belief") in order to view the biblical text with fresh eyes, as if they were studying the Koran or the Upanishads. It was easier for them than for their ancestors because of the influence upon them of Protestant Rationalism, which, for instance, rejected any belief in miracles.

But in all this, not surprisingly, there remained a residual tendency towards theological systemizing in the twentieth century among those who saluted the Biblical Theology and Neo-Orthodox banners, such as Anglican scholar Archibald M. Hunter. In their many books they seemed ready to recognize that various biblical authors had different beliefs, but they always ended up synthesizing them into a single "New Testament theology" or "Biblical theology."

More recently, scholars seem less eager to fuse the various Bible writers' belief-sets or systems, focusing instead on the distinctive voices for their own sakes. Even this, however, can be seen as a vestige of Protestant theology, since Protestants have always operated with a "canon within the canon," making Paul the chief authority. Luther was willing to thin out the New Testament canon, including only those gospels and epistles that he judged to adequately "convey Christ" (i.e., the Lutheran doctrine of justification by grace through faith). James, Jude, Revelation, and Hebrews were left on the cutting room floor. As Jerry Seinfeld once quipped, if you've got Superman, why do you need the rest of the Justice League? And, perhaps surprisingly, Luther's Superman was not Jesus, but Paul. After all, good luck finding justification by faith in the gospels! ("You know the commandments. Do this and you will live."). So if other New Testament writers do not measure up to the Great Apostle, so what? Who needs 'em? But you don't have to tear those pages out of your Bible; just ignore them.

Today's New Testament scholars don't ignore the non-Pauline letters: after all, they need grist for their mills. You've got to have *some*thing to write dissertations about, right? But Paul is still where the action is. So there remains an urgency to exposit, to systematize, "Pauline theology," as if it were still important for one's residual Christian identity. This accounts, in my opinion, for the stubborn refusal to consider critical theories that question or deny the unity of the Pauline epistles, whether individually or as a group. Similarly, if the gospels wind up having different Christ-concepts we cannot harmonize with one another, that is relatively unimportant since only Pauline Christology is to be deemed normative.

Seemingly Seamless?

Form criticism of the gospels is based on the hypothesis that the evangelists were something like Al Bukhari, al-Muslim, and others who sifted through an ocean of oral traditions about the Prophet Muhammad, what he said and did, in order to compile a detailed guide to proper Islamic belief and practice. Their materials, the hadith they considered authentic, were complied into compendia, but not into narratives, not until Ibn-Ishaq produced his massive biography of Muhammad about a century after the Prophet's death. Gospel form critics saw the gospels as pretty much like that: mini-narratives (pericopes) stitched together to form a continuous mega-narrative. But they let some inconsistencies slide; they may not even have noticed them any more than pious gospel readers do today. I know *I* never did. For instance, Mark 12:35–37 flatly refutes the traditional notion that the coming Messiah would be a Davidic descendant, while Mark 10:46–52 depicts Bartimaeus hailing Jesus as "Son of David" with no apparent discomfort on the evangelist's part. The exegetical gymnastics performed by scholars to solve this problem are truly pathetic to witness. It is simply an inconsistency that Mark failed to notice. But the scholars cannot afford to admit it. Why not? Because they are hell-bent on establishing a definitive system of "Markan Christology." And to do that, you've got to do what Mark manifestly neglected to do, namely iron out his sources into a seemingly seamless garment.

If we want to exonerate ourselves as gospel interpreters we may have to drop the precious but nowadays hidden assumption, held over from centuries-old theology, that "scripture speaks with a single voice." Otherwise, the single voice you find there will be your own: exegesis as ventriloquism. I, however, am ready to venture forth, giving all the anomalous fragments their full voice. You see, I have for some time noticed that this and that saying or episode in each gospel, considered on its own, reads more naturally in a different sort of context from that in which we now find it embedded. And sometimes the particular character of the anomalous pericope suggests it would be more at home, it would make more natural sense, in a very different kind of Jesus story.

What I will be trying here is a modest attempt to go one step further than three of my favorite contemporary New Testament scholars: Helmut Koester, James M. Robinson,[1] and Burton L. Mack.[2] Koester and Robinson, star disciples of Rudolf Bultmann, put together a great book called *Trajectories through Early Christianity* (1971). The essays in the collection embodied a new methodology, tracing the development of early Christian literary genres back and forth between existing canonical documents and other slightly later works. For instance, the fact that the Gospel of Thomas unearthed in Nag Hammadi, Egypt, in 1945 is a collection of sayings attributed to Jesus, with scarcely a narrative element in sight (much like the Book of Proverbs, the Sentences of Sextus, the Wisdom of Solomon, and the Wisdom of Sirach), strengthens the plausibility of the theory that Matthew and Luke both used an

---

1. James M. Robinson and Helmut Koester, *Trajectories through Early Christianity* (Philadelphia: Fortress Press, 1971).

2. Burton L. Mack, *A Myth of Innocence: Mark and Christian Origins* (Philadelphia: Fortress Press, 1988).

analogous text, which scholars call "Q" (for *Quelle*, "source"), also a collection of contextless Jesus aphorisms. Further, Thomas forces us to consider whether there might have been some branch of pro-to-Christianity that understood Jesus simply as a wandering sage, a Jewish Socrates. If the compliers of Q and Thomas held Jesus as Messiah and Savior, they had a funny way of showing it. We have no right to assume and assert that they *must* have believed all the doctrines Paul, John, and Ignatius did. As Jacob Neusner[3] used to say, "What we cannot show, we do not know."

The Nag Hammadi library also contained various resurrection dialogues featuring a kind of news conference with the risen Jesus fielding questions from the disciples. In this way Gnostics sought to explain the "genuine" Jesus pedigree of esoteric teachings unattested in the canonical gospels. And yet reading these books allows us to understand what is really going on in the Last Supper discourses in the Gospel of John: chapter after chapter of teaching prompted by the disciples' queries. Robinson[4] recognized what was happening here: the Last Supper Discourses were resurrection dialogues pushed back before the crucifixion! Why? It is even better to put your esoteric teaching into the mouth of the *pre-Easter* Jesus.

The "trajectories" method is independently on display in Dennis R. MacDonald's *The Legend and the Apostle* (1983).[5] By bringing the apocryphal Acts of Paul to bear on 1 Corinthians chapter 7 and the Pastoral Epistles, MacDonald is able to throw a veritable flood of light upon some hitherto very puzzling passages, which, as it turns out, are concerned with the widespread early Christian

3. Jacob Neusner, *Rabbinic Literature & the New Testament: What We Cannot Show, We Do Not Know* (Valley Forge: Trinity Press International, 1994).

4. James M. Robinson, "On the Gattung of Mark (and John)," in David G. Buttrick, ed., *Jesus and Man's Hope*, Vol. I (Pittsburgh: Pittsburgh Theological Seminary, 1970), pp. 111–112.

5. Dennis Ronald MacDonald, *The Legend and the Apostle: The Battle for Paul in Story and Canon* (Philadelphia: Westminster John Knox Press, 1983).

practice of *encratism*, the gospel of celibacy even within marriage. Once you read the later texts you discover the meaning of earlier ones which are seen to belong to the same trajectory.

Burton Mack takes a similar approach in his books *A Myth of Innocence: The Gospel of Mark and Christian Origins* (1988) and *The Lost Gospel: The Book of Q and Christian Origins* (1994).[6] Following the lead of Robinson and Koester, Mack delineates several "Christ cults" and "Jesus movements" who would have elaborated the myth and character of Jesus in various directions given the needs and nature of each very different group. Some, once again, cherished Jesus as a Cynic philosopher, with no reference to cross or resurrection. Others proclaimed the imminent dawn of the Kingdom of God and thus viewed Jesus as the apocalyptic Son of Man. Others practiced their Christ faith as a sacramental Mystery Religion. And there were more. In all this, Mack is basically enlarging the scope of the traditional *Sitz-im-Leben* (life-setting, originary context) in which any particular story or saying arose, and what issue relevant to that community seems to have occasioned the creation of the pericope, whether that saying/story originated with a historical Jesus or with prophets and protégés speaking in his name. But the form critics took it pericope by pericope, taking for granted a vague but largely traditional ecclesiastical context. What Mack is doing is to imagine/reconstruct whole species of proto-Christianities inferred not from discrete units of gospel traditions, but rather by whole *Gattungs* or genres. Elaine Pagels[7] was doing essentially the same thing, extrapolating from the Nag Hammadi scriptures what sort of believing communities lay behind them. She seems to be unique in treating these Gnostic documents as the scriptures of living religions. And Mack is engaged in the same work, only in the adjacent field.

Here's my innovation (whether forward or backward, you decide). I will be outlining eight different types of ancient religious

---

6. Burton L. Mack, *The Lost Gospel: The Book of Q and Christian Origins* (San Francisco: HarperOne, 1994).

7. Elaine Pagels, *The Gnostic Gospels* (New York: Vintage Books, 1980).

narratives, each a function of a different sect or type of religion. I will briefly describe the social/theological context in which various gospel passages seem to belong. Then I will string out the plot trajectory like a clothesline and clothespin along it various summaries and quotations from non-biblical sources next to the "aberrant" gospel passages (drawn from any and all gospels) that seem to fit the story better. You see, like my esteemed predecessors, I think there were several types of pre-Christianity, but also that each had a very different Jesus story, different not only from one another but also from the canonical gospels. These implicit narratives are what I am calling "the gospels behind the gospels."

In accord with *Trajectories in Early Christianity* and *A Myth of Innocence*, I want to peer beneath the surface of the canonical gospels. We may stand to discover some pretty interesting things if we abandon the logocentric approach whereby we have assumed each gospel writer had and set forth his own Christology. This approach produced harmonizations in the name of synthesis. But various texts continue to expose the hoax. What I propose is that each evangelist employed bits and pieces from prior Jesus stories in new and inconsistent combinations. But if we start to do some archaeological delving beneath the familiar surface layer, we may unearth earlier pictures, i.e., understandings, of Jesus that were consistent throughout and which conformed to different genres of which only incongruent vestiges remain in the "official," canonical texts. Bruce Chilton has famously declared "A text is not a tel."[8] But maybe he's wrong. Hand me that pick and shovel!

---

8. That is, an archaeological site to be exposed layer by layer.

1

JOHN THE BAPTIST REDIVIVUS

In Mark 8:27–28 Jesus' disciples inform him of the leading estimates of him held by segments of his public. The fact that there even *is* such a range of opinions is striking: Jesus cannot have been teaching anything about his identity. This reticence is of course part and parcel of Mark's redactional device of the Messianic Secret. But it is no less intriguing to speculate as to what those people believed beyond the proposed name tags of John the Baptizer, Elijah, and a prophet of old. I believe these three designations represent rival "Christologies" current in the Markan evangelist's day. Yes, he means to set forth his own Christology that Jesus was/ is the Christ, the Anointed Messiah. But he could have done that without putting up, then knocking down, the three "false" options. It makes more sense if he was trying to refute a trio of "heretical" Christological opinions held by some contemporaries, perhaps actually current at Caesarea Philippi. It makes me wonder if Mark and other canonical evangelists have repurposed various materials, major or minor, from the surviving rival sects who likewise revered Jesus, but as identified as John the Baptist, Elijah, or the Prophet like Moses (see below).[9] Accordingly, I suspect the Transfiguration

This chapter is a slightly tweaked version of the essay originally published in my collection, *Jesus Is Dead* (Cranford: American Atheist Press, 2007), pp. 75–90.

9. The Gospel of Thomas, saying 13, retells the same story to serve

scene (Mark 9:2–8) attempts to rebut both the rival Moses and Elijah Christologies. That would be the point of the divine Voice choosing Jesus as his favorite, not Moses, not Elijah. In the present chapter I want to begin taking them one by one, lining up the surviving traditions salvaged from these cousin sects.

Naturally, I do not and cannot claim that any of these pioneer scholars would second the motions I am making here. I admire their work and hope my crazed meanderings here will not embarrass them. Of course, Drs. Koester and Mack are gone, residing now in the Higher-Critical Valhalla. Dr. Robinson is still with us to catch the flack.

Jesus before Easter?

Some scholars have suggested that the apparent cleavage between the pre-Easter Jesus and the Risen Christ is an optical illusion in the sense that even before the Passion and Resurrection Jesus is already depicted thoroughly transformed by and into the Christological image of the Church's faith. The sayings attributed to Jesus seem for the most part to have arisen within the early Christian communities to address the needs of those communities. It is not as if we have the historical Jesus up till the Passion, followed by the Christ of faith as of Easter morning. No, it is the voice of Christian wisdom and prophecy which speaks the logia of the gospels. The situation of the canonical gospels is essentially no different

---

its own purposes; Thomas substitutes competing Christologies current in his own milieu, namely the angel Christology familiar from various Jewish-Christian sources (See, e.g., Darrell D. Hannah [not the mermaid], *Michael and Christ: Michael Tradition and Angel Christology in Early Christianity* (Eugene, OR: Wipf & Stock, 2011)) and the sage "Christ-"ology of the earliest stratum of the Q document, which seems to have viewed Jesus as a Cynic-type wise man like Diogenes, not as a martyred Son of God. For this see Mack, *Lost Gospel*, pp. 67–69, 73–74; John Dominic Crossan, *The Historical Jesus: The Life of a Mediterranean Jewish Peasant* (San Francisco: HarperOne, 1993), chapter 4, "Poverty and Freedom," pp. 72–88; David Seeley, "Jesus and the Cynics Revisited." *Journal of Biblical Literature*. Vol. 116, no. 4, 1997, pp. 704–712.

from that of the Gnostic resurrection dialogues in this respect: all the teaching ascribed to Jesus is attributable to the early Christians, as Norman Perrin[10] and James M. Robinson[11] make clear. Darrell J. Doughty even goes so far as to suggest that the whole of the Gospel of Mark's "pre-Easter" period is in fact identical with the post-Easter period, the result of a circular structure whereby the meeting of the disciples with Jesus on the shore of Galilee in Mark 1:16–17 is the fulfillment of the words of the angel in Mark 16:7 that they should meet him there.

If we are to take all this seriously, an obvious question presents itself: what of the original, historical, pre-Easter Jesus? He is not simply to be identified with the character of Jesus of Nazareth in the gospels (as naively presupposed in the title of Juan Luis Segundo's *The Historical Jesus of the Synoptics*).[12] Has he been altogether lost from the gospel narrative then? Perhaps not. Let us for a brief moment think the unthinkable. Suppose the figure of the pre-Easter Jesus is to be found under the alias of John the Baptist. When we impose this outlandish paradigm onto the gospels, we get some interesting results. A number of things make new sense.

Thy Kingdom Come

First, there's the sequential progression from John's ministry of repentance and asceticism, from which Jesus' style notoriously differed. Historical Jesus scholars commonly say that Jesus discerned that some great corner had been turned. Something signaled that the anticipated kingdom had now arrived, and that fasting was no longer appropriate. And thus he broke with John's ministry of penitential preparation for the kingdom and began a ministry cel-

---

10. Norman Perrin, *What Is Redaction Criticism?* Fortress Guides to Biblical Criticism (Philadelphia: Fortress Press, 1969), pp. 74–79.

11. Robinson, "On the Gattung of Mark (and John)," pp. 51–98.

12. Juan Luis Segundo, *The Historical Jesus of the Synoptics: 2. Jesus of Nazareth Yesterday and Today.* Trans. John Drury (Maryknoll: Orbis Books, 1985).

ebrating the kingdom's advent. Instead of fasting with the Pharisees (like John's disciples, Mark 2:18) he began feasting with the publicans. What could that momentous event have been? What could have signaled the shift of the eons? Nothing we see in the gospels, at least not on any straightforward or any traditional reading. Scholars just approach the texts taking for granted the Christological solution that, since Jesus was divine, he knew God's plan, so he happened to know the crucial page had been turned.

But suppose the transition was something quite specific, namely his own death and (supposed) resurrection. This would have signaled the disciples, not Jesus himself, that the corner had been turned. Had we listened to Bultmann, we would have remembered that the pericope must in any case refer to the practice of Christians, not that of Jesus himself, since the critics ask concerning *their* behavior, not *his*. "Good Christian men, rejoice, with heart and soul and voice. He calls you one and calls you all to share his everlasting hall. He hath opened heaven's door, and man shall live forever more." Thus the difference between John's mournful, fasting disciples and Jesus' feasting disciples is that between the same group before and after the Passion Week. "John's" disciples are already fasting because the bridegroom has been taken away from them (Mark 2:19–20), but once he is restored unto them at the resurrection, they rejoice again. No more fasting.

In a Looking Glass Darkly

Mark 1:14 ("And after John had been delivered up, Jesus came into Galilee, preaching the gospel of God.") has Jesus neatly replace John on the public stage, occasioning the popular opinion that Jesus' public advent signaled the miraculous return of John. Note the use of *paradidomi*, the same pregnant word used for the sacrificial delivering up of Jesus to death, whether by God (Rom. 8:32) or by Judas Iscariot (Mark 3:19). Can the same delivering up, i.e., of the same man, be in view? To say that John was delivered up and that Jesus appeared in Galilee immediately afterward would be like saying that the historical Jesus was delivered up for our sins and that shortly thereafter the Christ of faith appeared on the scene.

Similarly, the Johannine statements (John 3:26 4:1) about the baptism of Jesus eclipsing that of John would refer, on the present hypothesis, to the new situation after Easter, when the sect of the historical Jesus is being transformed, not without some resistance on the part of "doubting Thomases," into the cult of the Risen Christ. "Lord, teach us to pray as John taught his disciples" (Luke 11:1) means that a new prayer is needed for the time of fulfillment, which has dawned. Perhaps the old prayer contained the petition "Thy kingdom come," whereas the new replaced it with "Send thy Spirit upon us and sanctify us" (as some manuscripts of Luke's version of the prayer at 11:2 still read) because the kingdom was believed now to have arrived.

Scholars have remarked how, despite the strong difference between the religious styles of the two men, Jesus continues to identify himself with John, as when he counters the chief priests' question as to his authority by asking their estimate of John's authorization (Mark 11:28–30). What if the answer to the one is the answer also to the other—because Jesus and John are the same? The authority of the Christian preaching of the Risen One is as authoritative as one was willing to admit the ministry of the Baptist (i.e., his own earthly ministry) was. Of course the present narrative setting of the question and counter-question is anachronistic, as is most of the gospel material. We may suggest that the original context of the passage was in debate between post-Easter disciples of John ("Jesus"), believers in the Risen Baptist, on the one hand, and disciples of John who remained suspicious about this strange new proclamation on the other. What credentials did the new preaching have in its favor? The response? What credentials did the original ministry of the Baptist have? It was faith in either case, wasn't it?

So too the taunts "John came neither eating nor drinking, and you say, 'He is a demoniac.' The Son of Man came eating and drinking, and you say, 'Look, a glutton and a drunk'" (Matt. 11:16–19). Traditionally this is supposed to mean that people found a reason not to repent at the preaching of either man. John was too holier-than-thou for some, while Jesus seemed not to adhere to the parsimonious stereotype in the eyes of others. Finding an excuse to discount the messengers, that generation evaded coming to grips with their common message. But is that really the most natural reading of the text? The "damned if you do, damned if you don't" logic would fit best if the two styles characterized the same figure in successive phases. "Okay, first I tried this and you wouldn't have it; so then I tried doing what you said, but you didn't like that either!"

Twin Resurrections

Note, too, the strange similarity between Mark's report that some believed Jesus was John raised from the dead, accounting for the miraculous powers at work in him, and the resurrection formula of Romans 1:3–4, which has Jesus designated Son of God by miraculous power by virtue of the resurrection of the dead. Note the parallel:

Romans 1:4	*Mark 6:14*
declared Son of God	John the Baptist
by power	powers are at work in him
by his resurrection from the dead	has been raised from the dead

Perhaps this strange similarity denotes an even stranger identity, a dim recollection of the fact that Jesus was the same as John, that he had taken on the name/epithet "Jesus," savior, only after the resurrection. Compare two archaic hymn-fragments, the Johannine prologue (John 1:1–7ff) and the Kenosis hymn (Phil. 2:6–11). It is striking that the first text names no figure other than John the Baptist, and that in portentous theological terms: "There came into being a man sent from God, named John." As all recognize, the subsequent denigration of John as merely a witness to the light but most certainly not the light itself, is a theological correction akin to that found in Matthew 11:11b ("Of all those born of women no one has arisen greater than John the Baptist ... yet I tell you that the least in the kingdom of heaven is greater than he."). Bultmann saw that the Johannine prologue hymn must originally have referred to the Baptist.

Now look at Philippians 2:6–11, where the redeemer figure is named only at the end, where we learn that he received the honorific name "Jesus" only upon his postmortem exaltation, something which Paul-Louis Couchoud[13] pointed out long ago. Note that according to the synthetic parallelism, "at the name of Jesus every knee should bow" matches "and every tongue confess that Jesus Christ is Lord," implying that "bowing the knee to" equals "confessing the lordship of." The object of both is "Jesus." This may seem to belabor the obvious except that it requires that the great name God gave him at the exaltation was not "Kyrios" as harmonizing exegesis tells us, but rather "Jesus." The hymn means to say not that a man already named Jesus was then given the title Lord, but that a hitherto-unnamed hero was then given the honorific name Jesus. Couchoud remarks, "The God-man does not receive the name Jesus till after his crucifixion. That alone, in my judgment, is fatal to the historicity of Jesus." Unless he had borne some other name previously, as Peter had formerly been called Simon. What had "Jesus'" name been previously? "His name is John" (Luke 1:63). The identification of the pre-exaltation hero as John the Baptist would satisfy the problem Couchoud left open—had the hero been nameless before his exaltation?

Couchoud was implying that the earlier version of the bestowal of the name "Jesus" had the naming take place as part of the post-mortem exaltation of this figure. Only subsequently was the bestowal of the name associated with the earthly life of Jesus,

13. Paul-Louis Couchoud, "The Historicity of Jesus: A Reply to Alfred Loisy," *Hibbert Journal*, XXXVI, 2, pp. 205–206.

namely at his conception (Matt. 1:21; Luke 1:31). We can easily fit Couchoud's hypothesis into the speculations of mainstream scholarship. Raymond E. Brown[14] points out how

> The same combined ideas that early Christian preaching had once applied to the resurrection (i.e., a divine proclamation, the begetting of God's Son, the agency of the Holy Spirit), and which Mark had applied to the baptism, are now applied to the conception of Jesus in the words of an angel's message to Joseph and to Mary (respectively, in Matthew and in Luke). And once the conception of Jesus has become the Christological moment, the revelation of who Jesus is begins to be proclaimed to an audience who come and worship (the magi, the shepherds), while others react with hostility (Herod in Matthew; those who contradict the sign in Luke 2:34). And thus the infancy stories have become truly an infancy gospel."

Brown might have included Käsemann's observation[15] that the confessions of Jesus' identity by the demons (Mark 1:24, 34; 3:11; 5:7) are retrojections of the acclamations of those under the earth mentioned in Philippians 2:10–11. The retrojection of the same motif into the infancy story is, as Brown implies, the demonic persecution of the baby king by the Azdahak-like Herod, who thus acknowledges the true messiahship of his rival. The granting of the glorious savior-name "Jesus" is part of this package. It, too, would have found a place at the end of the savior's earthly life and been retrojected, along with the rest of the package, into the infancy. Once this happened, the identity of John and "Jesus" would have been severed and forever obscured.

Luke contains completely parallel accounts of the miraculous nativity of both figures, so close that even ancient scribes seem to have confused whether Zechariah was talking about the infant

---

14. Raymond E. Brown, *The Birth of the Messiah: A Commentary on the Infancy Narratives in Matthew and Luke* (Garden City: Doubleday 1977), p. 31.

15. Ernst Käsemann, *Jesus Means Freedom*. Trans. Frank Clarke (Philadelphia: Fortress Press, 1969), p. 56.

John or the infant Jesus (what is the reference to "the horn of salvation in the house of David" doing in a hymn about the Levitical John the Baptist?), and equally whether it was Elizabeth or Mary who sings the Magnificat (some ancient manuscripts of Luke 1:46 have "And Elizabeth said," while others read, "And she said.").

Splitting the Difference

More telling still is the parallel between the martyrdoms of Jesus and John, for both are put to death by a strangely reluctant profane tyrant, Jesus by Pontius Pilate, and John by Herod Antipas. But wait a moment; as Loisy[16] pointed out, Luke, like the Gospel of Peter, seems to have known a version of the Jesus martyrdom in which it was Herod Antipas who condemned Jesus to death! (He has harmonized it with Mark only with difficulty, having Antipas first desirous of killing Jesus, then acquitting him, but nonetheless remanding him to Pilate!) Perhaps this is because they were the same.

How on earth could the single figure have been bifurcated? Simple: there remained a dour penitential sect devoted to the martyred John which continued to anticipate the coming of the kingdom with (ascetic) observance (Luke 17:20), while another group of John's disciples came to believe he had been raised from the dead, as the first fruits, ushering in the kingdom, albeit invisibly. These bestowed on John the title "Yeshua," for he had saved his people from their sins. In time this became a name, just as "Iscariot" and "Peter" did, finally supplanting the original name, except among those who had never embraced the title and Christology of "Jesus." Thus in time people began to imagine that John and Jesus had been two different contemporary figures, though the rivalry between them was vaguely recalled. On the basis of it, e.g., Mandaeans rejected Jesus as a false messiah, though they did not deem John, their prophet, the true messiah! (This honor they reserved

16. Alfred Loisy, *The Origins of the New Testament*. Trans. L.P. Jacks (London: George Allen and Unwin, 1950), p. 167.

for Enosh-Uthra, a heavenly angel.) On the other hand, the first Christians were those who wondered in their hearts whether John himself were perhaps the Christ (Luke 3:15) and decided he was. He was the Jesus, the Christ.

A notorious problem text in Acts is the introduction of Apollos, who is confusingly said to have preached accurately the things concerning Jesus, yet knowing only the baptism of John. Priscilla and Aquila then set him straight in some unspecified way (Acts 18:24–28). All sorts of reconstructions have been advanced, many of them making Apollos a kind of half-Christian. How could he have correctly understood Jesus and yet known only John's baptism, when the main point about Jesus, at least with respect to John, was that he superseded John and made his baptism superfluous? But what if Luke's source preserves the fossil recollection that to know accurately the things about Jesus was precisely to know the baptism of John, since "Jesus" was none other than the resurrected John?[17]

Narrative Mitosis

Is the whole thing utterly implausible? If an historical analogy would help, recall F.C. Baur's theory that Simon Magus was a bifurcated "evil twin" of the Apostle Paul. Simon Magus was at first a caricature of Paul understood as a usurping opponent of Simon Peter, a false pretender to apostleship who sought to purchase the recognition by the Pillars by means of the collection made among the Gentile churches (compare Acts 8:18–24 with Galatians 2:7–10). As time went by, Simon Magus was imagined to be a separate figure from Paul. Later anti-Paulinists no longer got the joke, so to speak, while the whole idea would have been lost on Paulinists from the start. Especially once Petrine and Pauline factions became Catholicized and harmonized with one another, the connection between Paul and Simon Magus was utterly severed, and

---

17. I owe this suggestion to my old Jesus Seminar colleague Arthur Dewey.

the two separate characters were established. Suppose something similar happened in the case of Jesus and John the Baptist, only in this case neither one was a caricature. The Baptist was simply the remembered "historical Jesus," while "Jesus the Christ" was John the Baptist believed resurrected and made both Jesus (i.e., Savior) and Messiah.

To translate the scenario envisioned here into more traditional terms, it is as if some admirers of the pre-Easter Jesus had later heard of a resurrected "Christ" and not known to connect this figure with their Jesus. They might have been found thinking that this new "Christos" they heard so much about was someone entirely distinct from their late, lamented master Jesus. In fact, a development something like this did take place in the case of "separationist" Gnostics who decided that the human Jesus had so tenuous a connection to the Christ that they might curse the former and bless the latter (1 Cor. 12:3; cf., Origen on the Cainite Gnostics).

Needless to say, it would only have been once the single original character had been doubled, and the Risen Savior historicized, that Jesus could be read back into the pre-Easter history alongside John the Baptist, and once this happens we have the bizarre spectacle of Jesus appearing at John's baptism, only in another sense it is no longer so problematical: naturally he is there! Where else would he be? Matthew's version (3:14) puts the problem in its most acute form but also provides a hint of the solution. "I need to be baptized by you! And do you come to me?" Most scholars think that the Fourth Gospel's depiction of Jesus having a baptismal ministry alongside John's is a piece of symbolic anachronism in which early Christian baptism is retrojected into the time of Jesus and John, as if to show the superiority of the Christian sect to John's. So far so good. What I am suggesting is that not only is the picture of Jesus baptizing alongside John an anachronistic retrojection; the whole idea of Jesus and John as distinct contemporaries is merely another facet of the same retrojection.

The Fourth Gospel has Simon, Andrew, and the Beloved Dis-

ciple already disciples of John the Baptist before they become followers of Jesus. Do they abandon the first master to follow a new
one? Not if the point is that they are following the same master
before and after Easter. Even on the conventional reading we can
well imagine Peter being called a disciple of Jesus before Easter
and a disciple of Christ afterward, and we can just as easily imagine someone hearing both and imagining Peter had transferred
allegiances somewhere along the line.

Shall We Look for Another?

Finally, consider the Q passage in which the imprisoned John
sends his messengers to ask Jesus whether he may not be the
Coming One John's preaching had anticipated (Matt. 11:2–6/
Luke 7:18–20, 22–23). John's question (actually Jesus hears it from
the disciples themselves) "Or should we wait for another?" implies
that the attribution of the question to John is secondary, just as
in all the gospel pericopes wherein Jesus is asked why his disciples flout this or that pious custom (Mark 2:18, 24). As Bultmann
asked, why not ask Jesus why *he* fails to eat with hands washed
(Mark 7:5), why *he himself* gleans on the sabbath (Mark 2:24), if
it is really Jesus himself who is in view. But it is not. He serves as
a figurehead for his community, whose prerogatives are actually at
stake. In just the same way it is not John's uncertainty of Jesus as
the Coming One that this Q pericope presupposes, but rather that
of his disciples, bereft following his martyrdom. Can they accept
the kerygmatic Risen One as the return of their master?

Albert Schweitzer (*The Mystery of the Kingdom of God*) understood the same passage along somewhat similar lines in that he
had Jesus and John applying the same eschatological role each to
the other. The Baptist sends his messengers to ask whether Jesus
may be the Coming One. Jesus sends the same messengers back
to John and tells the crowd that John is himself the Coming One,
Elijah (Matt. 11:10/Luke 7:27). The scene can be read as a dou-
blet: Jesus = John, so the two sendings of the Baptist disciples are

the same. And these "sent ones" are apostles bearing the tidings of the Coming One who has arrived: call him Jesus or call him John, it is all the same.

Finally, if the case set forth here is judged plausible, it would provide the answer to a thorny question aimed at the Christ Myth theory nowadays dismissed out of hand by apologists and even some skeptics but still beloved by many freethinkers. It is easy to show that, at least in its most famous form, the testimony of Josephus to Jesus is a Christian interpolation. But no such case can be made in respect of Josephus' reference to John's baptism and his fate at the hands of Antipas. So apologists have asked, is it really likely that Jesus was not a historical figure but that John the Baptist was? That is exactly the implication if John the Baptist was the original "Jesus," and if the gospel Jesus is a figment of faith in the resurrected John. Only now it makes sense. That John should be a historical figure and Jesus a myth makes plenty of sense once you understand the relationship between the two figures as I have sketched it here.

2

ELIJAH/ELISHA RETURNED

I am including Elisha materials along with Elijah traditions. The two characters are hard to distinguish. Even the close and confusing similarity of their names hints at the possibility that the two heroes were originally the same. But this is not so. Back in the beginning, both were celestial symbols.[18] Elijah was the personified sun, as is still obvious from the clues surviving as fossils even in the present text. Elijah was (like the similarly hirsute Esau and Samson and lion-mane-wearing Hercules) a "hairy man" (literal reading of 2 Kgs. 1:8). He summons fire from heaven (1 Kgs, 18:38; 2 Kgs. 1:10, 12). He ascends to the zenith of the heavens in a fiery chariot like his Greek counterpart Apollo, 2 Kgs. 2:11. For his part, Elisha (like Abraham, father of the multitude of stars, and the "smooth man" Jacob) is the moon, symbolized by his bald dome (2 Kgs. 2:23). As the moon follows the sun in the sky, Elisha succeeds Elijah on the stage. In any case, once they became narratized into (super)human heroes, Elijah and Elisha serve as twin instantiations of the same actantial role, which is why you can hardly tell them apart..

Mark (6:14–15; 8:28) reports the belief of one faction of those interested in Jesus that, though actually named "Jesus" ("for his

---

18. Ignaz Goldziher, *Mythology Among the Hebrews and its Historical Development.* Trans. Russell Martineau (New York: Washington Square Publishers, 1967), pp. 167–168.

name had become known," Mark 6:14a) he was in reality the prophetically anticipated Elijah. This might imply that they expected Jesus to prepare the way for the Messiah. Albert Schweitzer thought that this was the belief of John the Baptizer concerning Jesus, even if Jesus regarded John himself as Elijah.[19] I am suggesting that, whatever the Baptizer, or Jesus, may or may not have believed, Mark attests that there were people who upheld the belief that Jesus was or had been the prophesied Elijah. As Geza Vermes noted,[20] this need not have meant that they believed Jesus-Elijah was the harbinger of the End, since ancient Jewish lore was replete with stories in which Elijah, monitoring earthly affairs from heaven, would occasionally "beam down" to rescue some pious person from a tight spot. If Jesus was believed to be a miracle-worker, such a version of Elijah "Christology" would make a lot of sense. Such miracles might not, in this belief, have been signs of the End.

Then again, it would also make sense if they *were*: if Elijah had returned to signal the verge of the Apocalypse, how would you know it was he? How to recognize him? The obvious way to authenticate one's identity as Elijah returned would be to do again the things Elijah once did. And this would fit the fact that several Jesus stories portray not just miracles per se, but specifically episodes modeled upon Old Testament tales of the Tishbite thaumaturge. As several scholars have observed, a number of pericopes in the gospels are almost certainly rewrites of Old Testament counterparts, notably those featuring Elijah and Elisha (as befitting their actantial unity). The point of such mimetic rewriting would have been to attest Jesus' identity as Elijah returned. Next I want to review several Elijah, then Elisha, stories, showing how each has been rewritten by those who believed Jesus had been the returned Elijah (and Elisha).

---

19. Albert Schweitzer, *The Mystery of the Kingdom of God: The Secret of Jesus' Messiahship and Passion*. Trans. Walter Lowrie (New York: Schocken Books, 1964), pp. 149–150.

20. Geza Vermes, *Jesus the Jew: A Historian's Reading of the Gospels* (London: Fontana/Collins, 1976), p. 90.

Wilderness Testing

Mark 1:12–13 relates how "The Spirit immediately drove him out into the wilderness. And he was in the wilderness forty days, tempted by Satan; and he was with the wild beasts; and the angels ministered to him." Some make much of the parallel between the forty *days* of Jesus in the wilderness and Moses' period of forty *years* in the desert of Midian before returning to Egypt,[21] but surely the Markan episode is closer to the forty-day retreat of Elijah to the wilderness after the contest with Baal's prophets in 1 Kings 19:5–8.

> And he lay down and slept under a broom tree; and behold, an angel touched him, and said to him, "Arise and eat." And he looked, and behold, there was at his head a cake baked on hot stones and a jar of water. And he ate and drank, and lay down again. And the angel of the LORD came again a second time, and touched him, and said, "Arise and eat, else the journey will be too great for you." And he arose, and ate and drank, and went in the strength of that food forty days and forty nights to Horeb the mount of God.

In the desert Elijah, like Jesus, is ministered unto by angels.[22] Notice that Elijah is not supposed to have been fasting during his eremitic sojourn. I should think Mark's version likewise means that Jesus, too, was supplied with food by the angels who "served" him. The version of the Temptation narrative shared by Matthew (4:1–11) and Luke (4:1–13) specifically says Jesus ate nothing (not even manna!) the whole time. We have been too quick to read the fasting into Mark's version.

---

21. Dale Miller and Patricia Miller, *The Gospel of Mark as Midrash on Earlier Jewish and New Testament Literature*. Studies in the Bible and Early Christianity 21 (Lewiston/Queenston/Lampeter: Edwin Mellen Press, 1990), p. 109.

22. John Bowman, *The Gospel of Mark: The New Christian Jewish Passover Haggadah*. Studia Post-Biblica 8. (Leiden: E.J. Brill, 1965), p. 48.

Echoes of Zarephath

The Synoptic Gospels preserve versions of a challenge to Jesus to perform some miracle to verify God's approval of his ministry (Mark 8:11–12; Luke 11:29–30; Matt. 12:38–41),[23] his critics perhaps envisioned as skeptical about rumors of previous wonders.[24] Jesus refuses, offering various, rather equivocal, excuses. My guess is that Luke 4:25–27 constitutes a similar evasion of complaints by skeptics: if Jesus is really the returned Elijah as he or some claim, why has he not performed miracles as the biblical Elijah (and Elisha) tales record?

> But in truth, I tell you, there were many widows in Israel in the days of Elijah, when the heaven was shut up three years and six months, when there came a great famine over all the land; and Elijah was sent to none of them but only to Zarephath, in the land of Sidon, to a woman who was a widow. And there were many lepers in Israel in the time of the prophet Elisha; and none of them was cleansed, but only Naaman the Syrian.

This wouldn't have satisfied anyone who harbored such doubts,

---

23. Jesus' reply in Mark is merely an abrupt refusal, questioning the motives of his opponents. By itself it seems to rule out the possibility of Jesus *ever* performing any miracles, since, a la Luke 16:31, they are not productive of faith anyway. In order to make room for the many miracle stories crowding all the gospels, even Mark's own, Luke 11:29–31 introduces an ambiguous qualifier somehow appealing to the example of Jonah. Matthew resolves the ambiguity by inserting a prediction of the resurrection (Matt. 12:40). A better resolution would have been the reply Jesus gives to Pilate in the Martin Scorsese and Paul Schrader film adaptation of Nikos Kazantzakis's *The Last Temptation of Christ*, when the procurator (stealing Herod Antipas' lines) requests a miracle and Jesus says, "I'm not a circus animal," i.e., to perform on demand.

24. Cf. Gershom Scholem, *Sabbatai Sevi: The Mystical Messiah 1626–1676*. Trans. R.J. Zwi Werblowsky. Bollingen Series XCIII (Princeton: Princeton University Press, 1973), p. 612: "In carefully guarded language the rabbis of Constantinople avow their perplexity: 'So far we have not beheld a single miracle or sign' from the messiah or from the prophet [Nathan] of Gaza, 'only the noise of rumors and testimonies at second hand.'"

so the believers in Jesus the Tishbite filled the gap by producing rewrites of the biblical originals, most of them based on the Zarephath story in 1 Kings 17:8–24 (LXX), in which Elijah rescues a destitute widow and her son in repayment for her generosity. Elijah miraculously multiplies food for her, providing a metaphor for how potent the story has been in its own literary multiplication into several dependent Jesus stories.

> And the word of the Lord came to Elijah saying, Arise, and go to Zarephath of the Sidonian land: behold, I have there commanded a widow-woman to maintain thee. And he arose and went to Zarephath, and came to the gate of the city: and, behold, a widow-woman was there gathering sticks; and Elijah cried after her, and said to her, Fetch me, I pray thee, a little water in a vessel that I may drink. And she went to fetch it; and Elijah cried after her, and said, Bring me, I pray thee, a morsel of the bread that is in thy hand. And the woman said, As the Lord thy God lives, I have not a cake, but only a handful of meal in the pitcher, and a little oil in the cruise, and, behold, I am going to gather two sticks, and I shall go in and dress it for myself and my children, and we shall eat it and die. And Elijah said to her, Be of good courage, go in and do according to thy word: but make me thereof a little cake, and thou shalt bring it out to me first, and thou shalt make some for thyself and thy children last. For thus saith the Lord, The pitcher of meal shall not fail, and the cruse of oil shall not diminish, until the day that the Lord gives rain upon the earth. And the woman went and did so, and did eat, she, and he, and her children. And the pitcher of meal failed not, and the cruse of oil was not diminished, according to the word of the Lord which he spoke by the hand of Elijah. And it came to pass afterward, that the son of the woman the mistress of the house was sick; and his sickness was very severe, until there was no breath left in him. And she said to Elijah, What have I to do with thee, O man of God? Hast thou come in to me to bring my sins to remembrance, and to slay my son? And Elijah said to the woman, Give me thy son. And he took him out of her bosom, and took him up to the chamber in which he himself lodged, and laid him on the bed. And Elijah cried aloud, and said, Alas, O Lord, the witness of the widow

with whom I sojourn, thou hast wrought evil for her in slaying her son. And he breathed on the child thrice, and called on the Lord, and said, O Lord my God, let, I pray thee, the soul of this child return to him. And it was so, and the child cried out, and he brought him down from the upper chamber into the house, and gave him to his mother; and Elijah said, See, thy son lives. And the woman said to Elijah, Behold, I know that thou art a man of God, and the word of the Lord in thy mouth is true.

John 2:1–12, the tale of Jesus turning water into wine, is but one Jesus version of the Widow of Zarephath story.

On the third day there was a marriage at Cana in Galilee, and the mother of Jesus was there; Jesus also was invited to the marriage, with his disciples. When the wine failed, the mother of Jesus said to him, "They have no wine." And Jesus said to her, "O woman, what have you to do with me? My hour has not yet come." His mother said to the servants, "Do whatever he tells you." Now six stone jars were standing there, for the Jewish rites of purification, each holding twenty or thirty gallons. Jesus said to them, "Fill the jars with water." And they filled them up to the brim. He said to them, "Now draw some out, and take it to the steward of the feast." So they took it. When the steward of the feast tasted the water now become wine, and did not know where it came from (though the servants who had drawn the water knew), the steward of the feast called the bridegroom and said to him, "Every man serves the good wine first; and when men have drunk freely, then the poor wine; but you have kept the good wine until now." This, the first of his signs, Jesus did at Cana in Galilee, and manifested his glory; and his disciples believed in him.

Though the central feature of this miracle story, the transformation of one liquid into another, no doubt comes from the lore of Dionysus, the basic outline of the story owes much to that of Elijah in 1 Kings 17:8–24 LXX.[25] The widow of Zarephath, whose

---

25. Randel Helms, *Gospel Fictions* (Buffalo: Prometheus Books, 1989), p. 86.

son has just died, upbraids the prophet: "What have I to do with you, O man of God?" (John has transferred this brusque address to the mouth of Jesus, rebuking his mother, 2:4). Jesus and Elijah both tell people in need of provisions to take empty pitchers (1 Kgs 17:12; John 2:6–7), which he will miraculously fill.

The story of the Samaritan Woman (John 4:1–42) is likewise based upon that of the widow of Zarephath. Elijah and Jesus alike leave their home turf for foreign territory. Each is thirsty and meets a woman of whom he asks a drink of water. The woman of Zarephath is a widow, while the Samaritan woman has given up on marriage, having had five previous husbands, now dead or divorced, and is presently just cohabiting. In both stories it is really the woman who stands in need more than the prophet, and the latter offers the boon of a miraculously self-renewing supply of nourishment, Elijah that of physical food, Jesus that of the water of everlasting life. Just as the widow exclaims that Elijah must have come to disclose her past sins: "You have come to me to bring my sin to remembrance" (1 Kgs 17:18), the Samaritan admits Jesus has the goods on her as well ("He told me all that I ever did," John 4:39).

The episode of Peter's mother-in-law (Mark 1:29–31), too, is cut from the cloth of Elijah's mantle.

> And immediately he left the synagogue, and entered the house of Simon and Andrew, with James and John. Now Simon's mother-in-law lay sick with a fever, and immediately they told him of her. And he came and took her by the hand and lifted her up, and the fever left her; and she served them.

This time the son of the helpless widow is associated with the prophet rather than with his mother. He has switched sides from the recipient of help to that of the giver of help.

The Syro-Phoenician Woman

When Jesus meets a foreign woman in the district of Tyre and Sidon, who requests his help for her child, we find ourselves back with Elijah and widow of Sidonian Zarephath. There the prophet Elijah encounters a foreign widow and performs a miracle for her and her son. In both cases the miracle is preceded by a tense interchange between the prophet and the woman in which he raises the bar to gauge the woman's faith. The Syrophoenician parries Jesus' initial dismissal with a clever comeback; the widow of Zarephath is bidden to take her remaining meal and to cook it up for Elijah first, whereupon the meal is indefinitely multiplied.[26] Why does Jesus call the poor woman and her daughter, by implication, dogs? It comes from 2 Kings 8:7–15, where Elisha tells Hazael (a Syrian, like the woman in Mark) that he will succeed Ben-Hadad to the throne of Aram. He replies, "What is your servant, the dog, that he should accomplish this great thing?" In the Jesus version the question is whether the great deed shall be done *for* the "dog."[27]

But we are still not done with the widow's tale, for it forms the basis for both that of the centurion's slave (or child)[28] and the son of the widow of Nain (Luke 7:1–17)

> After he had ended all his sayings in the hearing of the people he entered Capernaum. Now a centurion had a slave who was dear to him, who was sick and at the point of death. When he heard of Jesus, he sent to him elders of the Jews, asking him to come and heal his slave. And when they came to Jesus, they besought him earnestly, saying, "He is worthy to have you do this for him, for he loves our nation, and he built us our synagogue." And Jesus went with them. When he was not far from the house, the centurion sent friends to him, saying to him, "Lord, do not trouble yourself, for I am not worthy to have you

---

26. Wolfgang Roth, *Hebrew Gospel: Cracking the Code of Mark* (Oak Park: Meyer-Stone Books, 1988), pp. 51–52; Miller, *Gospel of Mark as Midrash*, pp. 196–197.

27. Roth, *Hebrew Gospel*, p. 44.

28. Same word in Greek.

come under my roof; therefore I did not presume to come to you. But say the word, and let my servant be healed. For I am a man set under authority, with soldiers under me: and I say to one, 'Go,' and he goes; and to another, 'Come,' and he comes; and to my slave, 'Do this,' and he does it." When Jesus heard this he marveled at him, and turned and said to the multitude that followed him, "I tell you, not even in Israel have I found such faith." And when those who had been sent returned to the house, they found the slave well.

Soon afterward he went to a city called Nain, and his disciples and a great crowd went with him. As he drew near to the gate of the city, behold, a man who had died was being carried out, the only son of his mother, and she was a widow; and a large crowd from the city was with her. And when the Lord saw her, he had compassion on her and said to her, "Do not weep." And he came and touched the bier, and the bearers stood still. And he said, "Young man, I say to you, arise." And the dead man sat up, and began to speak. And he gave him to his mother. Fear seized them all; and they glorified God, saying, "A great prophet has arisen among us!" and "God has visited his people!" And this report concerning him spread through the whole of Judea and all the surrounding country.

First Kings 17 forms the basis for the two-miracle sequence here.[29] The original Elijah version stipulates (1 Kgs 17:1) how the famine shall be relieved only by the prophetic word, just as the mere word of Jesus is enough to heal the centurion's servant/child at a distance (Luke 7:7b). Elijah journeys to the Transjordan where he will meet a Gentile, the widow of Zarephath (1 Kgs 17:5, 10a), just as Jesus arrives in Capernaum to encounter a Roman centurion. Both Gentiles are in dire need, the widow about to succumb to starvation with her son (17:12), the centurion desperate to avert his son/slave's imminent death (7:2–3). Once the facts are made known to the miracle worker, there is a series of commands (1

---

29. Thomas L. Brodie, "Luke the Literary Interpreter: Luke-Acts as a Systematic Rewriting and Updating of the Elijah-Elisha Narrative in 1 and 2 Kings." Ph.D. dissertation presented to Pontifical University of St. Thomas Aquinas, Rome. 1988, pp. 136–137.

Kgs 17:10c–13; Luke 7:8), and divine deliverance is secured, the multiplication of food in the one case (17:6), the return of health in the other (7:10).

The Widow of Nain's son episode is modeled upon the 1 Kings sequel to the story of Elijah and the widow. Whereas Elijah later raises the widow's son from the dead, Jesus next comes upon a funeral procession and raises the man about to be buried, again a widow's son, this time from Nain. One feature from the first Elijah episode appears in this second Jesus episode: the initial meeting with the widow at the city gate of Zarephath, which he makes the gate of Nain (even though historical Ain had no gate).

The second episode commences with the same opening from 1 Kings 17:17a: "And it happened afterward" // "after this . . ." The widow's son is dead (1 Kgs. 17:17b; Luke 7:12b). Elijah cried out in anguish (1 Kgs. 17:19–20), unlike Jesus, who, however, tells the widow not to cry (Luke 7:13). After a gesture (Elijah prays for the boy's spirit to return, v. 21; Jesus commands the boy to rise, 7:14), the dead rises, proving his reanimation by crying out (1 Kgs. 17:22; Luke 7:15). His service rendered, the wonder-worker "gave him to his mother" (1 Kgs. 17:24; Luke 7:15b, verbatim identical). Those present glorify the hero (1 Kgs. 17:24; Luke 7:16–17).

Chain Lightning

In Mark's gospel we find two versions of a linked sequence of miracles and sayings.[30] The first version consists of Mark 4:35–41 (Stilling the Storm), 5:1–20 (Gadarene Demoniac), 5:21–43 (Woman with a Hemorrhage combined with Jairus' Daughter), and 6:34–44 (Feeding the 5,000). The second miracle chain is made up of Mark 6:45–51 (Walking on Water), 7:24–31 (The Syro-Phoenician Woman), 7:32–37 (Healing the Deaf-Mute), 8:1–

---

30. Paul J. Achtemeier, *Jesus and the Miracle Tradition* (Eugene, OR: Cascade Books, 2008), Chapter 4, "Toward the Isolation of Pre-Markan Miracle Catenae," pp. 55–86; Chapter 5, "The Origin and Function of the Pre-Markan Catenae," pp. 87–116.

10 (Feeding the 4,000), and 8:22–26 (Healing the Blind Man). The order is not precisely parallel, but that could be the result of variation during transmission or of Markan redaction. But it is plain that, first, there is a pair of sea miracles; second, a pair of exorcisms; third, a pair of pairs of healing miracles; fourth, a pair of miraculous feedings. The two miracle catenae are neither Davidic nor even Messianic. Whoever compiled the Markan miracle sequences certainly understood Jesus as Elijah/Elisha redivivus, not the Messiah.

Healing the Paralytic (2 Kings 1:2–17a; Mark 2:1–12)

Now Ahaziah fell through the lattice in his upper chamber in Samaria, and lay sick; so he sent messengers, telling them, "Go, inquire of Baal-zebub, the god of Ekron, whether I shall recover from this sickness." But the angel of the LORD said to Elijah the Tishbite, "Arise, go up to meet the messengers of the king of Samaria, and say to them, 'Is it because there is no God in Israel that you are going to inquire of Baal-zebub, the god of Ekron?' Now therefore thus says the LORD, 'You shall not come down from the bed to which you have gone, but you shall surely die.'" So Elijah went. The messengers returned to the king, and he said to them, "Why have you returned?" And they said to him, "There came a man to meet us, and said to us, 'Go back to the king who sent you, and say to him, Thus says the LORD, Is it because there is no God in Israel that you are sending to inquire of Baal-zebub, the god of Ekron? Therefore you shall not come down from the bed to which you have gone, but shall surely die.'" He said to them, "What kind of man was he who came to meet you and told you these things?" They answered him, "He wore a garment of haircloth, with a girdle of leather about his loins." And he said, "It is Elijah the Tishbite." Then the king sent to him a captain of fifty men with his fifty. He went up to Elijah, who was sitting on the top of a hill, and said to him, "O man of God, the king says, 'Come down.'" But Elijah answered the captain of fifty, "If I am a man of God, let fire come down from heaven and consume you and your fifty." Then fire came down from heaven, and consumed him and his fifty. Again the king sent to him another captain of fifty men with his fifty.

And he went up and said to him, "O man of God, this is the
king's order, 'Come down quickly!'" But Elijah answered them,
"If I am a man of God, let fire come down from heaven and
consume you and your fifty." Then the fire of God came down
from heaven and consumed him and his fifty. Again the king
sent the captain of a third fifty with his fifty. And the third
captain of fifty went up, and came and fell on his knees before
Elijah, and entreated him, "O man of God, I pray you, let my
life, and the life of these fifty servants of yours, be precious in
your sight. Lo, fire came down from heaven, and consumed the
two former captains of fifty men with their fifties; but now let
my life be precious in your sight." Then the angel of the LORD
said to Elijah, "Go down with him; do not be afraid of him." So
he arose and went down with him to the king, and said to him,
"Thus says the LORD, 'Because you have sent messengers to inquire of Baal-zebub, the god of Ekron,—is it because there is no
God in Israel to inquire of his word?—therefore you shall not
come down from the bed to which you have gone, but you shall
surely die.'" So he died according to the word of the LORD
which Elijah had spoken.

And when he returned to Capernaum after some days, it was re-
ported that he was at home. And many were gathered together,
so that there was no longer room for them, not even about the
door; and he was preaching the word to them. And they came,
bringing to him a paralytic carried by four men. And when they
could not get near him because of the crowd, they removed the
roof above him; and when they had made an opening, they let
down the pallet on which the paralytic lay. And when Jesus saw
their faith, he said to the paralytic, "My son, your sins are forgiven." Now some of the scribes were sitting there, questioning
in their hearts, "Why does this man speak thus? It is blasphemy!
Who can forgive sins but God alone?" And immediately Jesus,
perceiving in his spirit that they thus questioned within themselves, said to them, "Why do you question thus in your hearts?
Which is easier, to say to the paralytic, 'Your sins are forgiven,'
or to say, 'Rise, take up your pallet and walk'? But that you may
know that the Son of man has authority on earth to forgive
sins"—he said to the paralytic— "I say to you, rise, take up your
pallet and go home." And he rose, and immediately took up

the pallet and went out before them all; so that they were all amazed and glorified God, saying, "We never saw anything like this!"

As Roth[31] shows, this story of a paralyzed man's friends tearing the thatch off a roof and lowering him to Jesus amid the crowd seems to be based on an Elijah story in 2 Kings 1:2–17a. King Ahaziah gains his affliction by falling from his roof through the lattice and languishes in bed. Mark's sufferer is already afflicted when he descends through the roof on his bed (pallet). He rises from his bed because whatever sin of his had earned him the divine judgment of paralysis was now pronounced forgiven on account of his friends' faith, though nothing is said of his own. King Ahaziah is pointedly *not* healed of his affliction because of his own pronounced lack of faith in the God of Israel: he had sent to the priests of the Philistine oracle god Baal-zebub to inquire as to his prospects. Elijah tells him he is doomed because of unbelief, a dismal situation reversed by Mark, who has Jesus grant forgiveness and salvation because of faith. The Baal-zebub element pops up in a later story: "And the scribes who came down from Jerusalem said, 'He is possessed by Beel-zebul, and by the prince of demons he casts out the demons'" (Mark 3:22).

But of course there is also a direct rejoinder to the Elijah passage in Luke 9:51–56.

When the days drew near for him to be received up, he set his face to go to Jerusalem. And he sent messengers ahead of him, who went and entered a village of the Samaritans, to make ready for him; but the people would not receive him, because his face was set toward Jerusalem. And when his disciples James and John saw it, they said, "Lord, do you want us to bid fire come down from heaven and consume them?" But he turned and rebuked them, and he said, "You do not know what manner of spirit you are of; for the Son of man came to save men's lives, not to destroy them." And they went on to another village.

---

31. Roth, *Hebrew Gospel*, p. 56.

This would, on my reading, also have been part of the Jesus /Elijah gospel, even though it seems to criticize the prophet, since the point would be, as in other cases, that Jesus, the returned Elijah, was an improvement on the original: "A greater than Elijah is here," i.e., "He's back and he's better!"

Walk This Way

First Kings 19:19–21 and Luke 9:59–62 share an unmistakable note of similarity.

> So he departed from there, and found Elisha the son of Shaphat, who was plowing, with twelve yoke of oxen before him, and he was with the twelfth. Elijah passed by him and cast his mantle upon him. And he left the oxen, and ran after Elijah, and said, "Let me kiss my father and my mother, and then I will follow you." And he said to him, "Go back again; for what have I done to you?" And he returned from following him, and took the yoke of oxen, and slew them, and boiled their flesh with the yokes of the oxen, and gave it to the people, and they ate. Then he arose and went after Elijah, and ministered to him.
>
> To another he said, "Follow me." But he said, "Lord, let me first go and bury my father." But he said to him, "Leave the dead to bury their own dead; but as for you, go and proclaim the kingdom of God." Another said, "I will follow you, Lord; but let me first say farewell to those at my home." Jesus said to him, "No one who puts his hand to the plow and looks back is fit for the kingdom of God."

The stories of Jesus calling Peter, Andrew, James, and John (Mark 1:16–20) and Levi (Mark 2:14) all seem to stem from Elijah summoning Elisha to become his disciple and successor. Elijah's throwing his mantle onto Elisha's shoulders would seem to anticipate his subsequent bequest of his authority to his successor, a literal "investiture." But Luke features[32] another discipleship paradigm which implicitly critiques the prototype. In Luke 9:59–62,

---

32. Brodie, "Luke the Literary Interpreter," pp. 216–227.

Jesus forbids what Elijah allows, that the new recruit should delay long enough to pay filial respects. Also, whereas plowing was for Elisha the worldly pursuit he must abandon for the prophetic ministry, for Luke plowing becomes the very metaphor for that ministry.

The Request of James and John

Now when the LORD was about to take Elijah up to heaven by a whirlwind, Elijah and Elisha were on their way from Gilgal. And Elijah said to Elisha, "Tarry here, I pray you; for the LORD has sent me as far as Bethel." But Elisha said, "As the LORD lives, and as you yourself live, I will not leave you." So they went down to Bethel. And the sons of the prophets who were in Bethel came out to Elisha, and said to him, "Do you know that today the LORD will take away your master from over you?" And he said, "Yes, I know it; hold your peace." Elijah said to him, "Elisha, tarry here, I pray you; for the LORD has sent me to Jericho." But he said, "As the LORD lives, and as you yourself live, I will not leave you." So they came to Jericho. The sons of the prophets who were at Jericho drew near to Elisha, and said to him, "Do you know that today the LORD will take away your master from over you?" And he answered, "Yes, I know it; hold your peace." Then Elijah said to him, "Tarry here, I pray you; for the LORD has sent me to the Jordan." But he said, "As the LORD lives, and as you yourself live, I will not leave you." So the two of them went on. Fifty men of the sons of the prophets also went, and stood at some distance from them, as they both were standing by the Jordan. Then Elijah took his mantle, and rolled it up, and struck the water, and the water was parted to the one side and to the other, till the two of them could go over on dry ground. When they had crossed, Elijah said to Elisha, "Ask what I shall do for you, before I am taken from you." And Elisha said, "I pray you, let me inherit a double share of your spirit." And he said, "You have asked a hard thing; yet, if you see me as I am being taken from you, it shall be so for you; but if you do not see me, it shall not be so." (2 Kgs 2:1–10)

And they were on the road, going up to Jerusalem, and Jesus was walking ahead of them; and they were amazed, and those who followed were afraid. And taking the twelve again, he began to tell them what was to happen to him, saying, "Behold, we are going up to Jerusalem; and the Son of man will be delivered to the chief priests and the scribes, and they will condemn him to death, and deliver him to the Gentiles; and they will mock him, and spit upon him, and scourge him, and kill him; and after three days he will rise." And James and John, the sons of Zebedee, came forward to him, and said to him, "Teacher, we want you to do for us whatever we ask of you." And he said to them, "What do you want me to do for you?" And they said to him, "Grant us to sit, one at your right hand and one at your left, in your glory." But Jesus said to them, "You do not know what you are asking. Are you able to drink the cup that I drink, or to be baptized with the baptism with which I am baptized?" And they said to him, "We are able." And Jesus said to them, "The cup that I drink you will drink; and with the baptism with which I am baptized, you will be baptized; but to sit at my right hand or at my left is not mine to grant, but it is for those for whom it has been prepared." And when the ten heard it, they began to be indignant at James and John. And Jesus called them to him and said to them, "You know that those who are supposed to rule over the Gentiles lord it over them, and their great men exercise authority over them. But it shall not be so among you; but whoever would be great among you must be your servant, and whoever would be first among you must be slave of all. For the Son of man also came not to be served but to serve, and to give his life as a ransom for many." (Mark 10:32–45)

This whole Markan episode comes right out of that of Elisha's request of Elijah just before his ascension. Only Mark's version reflects badly on James and John. The structure is exactly the same.[33] Just as Elijah has (a bit surreptitiously) announced his departure three times, Jesus has just announced for the third time his impending death and resurrection, prompting the brothers to venture, "Teacher, we want you to do for us whatever we may ask of

---

33. Miller, *Gospel of Mark as Midrash*, p. 253.

you . . . Grant that we may sit in your glory, one at your right, one at your left" (Mark 10:35, 37). This comes from 2 Kings 2:9, "Ask what I shall do for you before I am taken from you." Hearing the request, Elijah reflects, "You have asked a hard thing" (v. 10), just as Jesus warns James and John, "You do not know what you are asking for." The Elijah-Elisha story cements the "apostolic succession" from one prophet to the other, whereas the corresponding Jesus version seems to pass over the two disciples to open the possibility of succession to anyone willing to follow Jesus, the new Elijah, along the way of martyrdom.

Elijah, Elijah, Why Have You Forsaken Me?

Originally Elijah was the sun personified, as several aspects of the Elijah stories in 1–2 Kings make clear. Note that when darkness has engulfed the land during Jesus' crucifixion, the bystanders think he is calling for Elijah. Does this preserve a folk memory that Elijah was the sun, and that Jesus is invoking him to restore the sunlight? Or that Jesus is lamenting that Elijah has withdrawn the sunlight?[34]

The Sun Also Rises

Does the ascension tradition clash with the resurrection? Does it imply an ascension of Jesus *without dying?* Such was the case, after all, with Apollonius, of whose departure many tales were told. The ascension narrative in Luke would be a remnant of the Elijah Christology. Elijah, after all, departed from the earth in a fiery chariot without dying. Of course, elsewhere in the New Testament Jesus' resurrection seems understood as a direct translation from

---

34. Levi Dowling, *The Aquarian Gospel of Jesus the Christ: The Philosophic and Practical Basis of the Religion of the Aquarian Age of the World* (Santa Monica: DeVorss & Co., 1907, 1972), 171:1–3, p. 252. "And when the sun refused to shine and darkness came, the Lord exclaimed, *Heloi! Heloi! Lama sabachthani (Thou sun! Thou sun! why hast thou forsaken me?)*" Elias=Helios.

the cross or the tomb to the throne next to God in heaven. But the logic of an ascension is that a still-living man levitates bodily and visibly into heaven. At least it seems so in many ancient myths. And so with the pouring out of the Spirit at Pentecost: like Elijah imparting a double share of his spirit to Elisha. Also, this fits with the earlier indications that Jesus survived crucifixion as Apollonius (and Elijah) did.

> A particularly strong influence on the Lucan ascension narratives comes from the Elijah traditions, esp. the link of the ascension with the subsequent outpouring of the Spirit, the emphasis on the visibility of the ascension, and the double function of their (Elijah's and Jesus') ascensions: it concludes the presence of the Master and at the same time (by virtue of the subsequent transfer of the Spirit) continues his ministry in the ministry of the successor. If we trace the comparison with Elijah a little further, it appears that in both cases their heavenly assumption is not the end, but inaugurates a period of temporal preservation in heaven with a view to a future eschatological return.[35]

Eleven Million Served

A man came from Baal-shalishah, bringing the man of God bread of the first fruits, twenty loaves of barley, and fresh ears of grain in his sack. And Elisha said, "Give to the men, that they may eat." But his servant said, "How am I to set this before a hundred men?" So he repeated, "Give them to the men, that they may eat, for thus says the LORD, 'They shall eat and have some left.'" So he set it before them. And they ate, and had some left, according to the word of the LORD. (2 Kgs 4:42–44)

The apostles returned to Jesus, and told him all that they had done and taught. And he said to them, "Come away by yourselves to a lonely place, and rest a while." For many were coming and going, and they had no leisure even to eat. And they went

35. A.W. Zwiep, *The Ascension of the Messiah in Lukan Christology.* Supplements to Novum Testamentum Vol. LXXXVII (New York: Brill, 1997), p. 116.

away in the boat to a lonely place by themselves. Now many saw them going, and knew them, and they ran there on foot from all the towns, and got there ahead of them. As he went ashore he saw a great throng, and he had compassion on them, because they were like sheep without a shepherd; and he began to teach them many things. And when it grew late, his disciples came to him and said, "This is a lonely place, and the hour is now late; send them away, to go into the country and villages round about and buy themselves something to eat." But he answered them, "You give them something to eat." And they said to him, "Shall we go and buy two hundred denarii worth of bread, and give it to them to eat?" And he said to them, "How many loaves have you? Go and see." And when they had found out, they said, "Five, and two fish." Then he commanded them all to sit down by companies upon the green grass. So they sat down in groups, by hundreds and by fifties. And taking the five loaves and the two fish he looked up to heaven, and blessed, and broke the loaves, and gave them to the disciples to set before the people; and he divided the two fish among them all. And they all ate and were satisfied. And they took up twelve baskets full of broken pieces and of the fish. And those who ate the loaves were five thousand men. (Mark 6:30–44)

In those days, when again a great crowd had gathered, and they had nothing to eat, he called his disciples to him, and said to them, "I have compassion on the crowd, because they have been with me now three days, and have nothing to eat; and if I send them away hungry to their homes, they will faint on the way; and some of them have come a long way." And his disciples answered him, "How can one feed these men with bread here in the desert?" And he asked them, "How many loaves have you?" They said, "Seven." And he commanded the crowd to sit down on the ground; and he took the seven loaves, and having given thanks he broke them and gave them to his disciples to set before the people; and they set them before the crowd. And they had a few small fish; and having blessed them, he commanded that these also should be set before them. And they ate, and were satisfied; and they took up the broken pieces left over, seven baskets full. And there were about four thousand people. And he sent them away; and immediately he got into the boat with his disciples, and went to the district of Dalmanutha. (Mark 8:1–10)

As all acknowledge, the basis for both the miraculous feeding stories in Mark's gospel is the story of Elisha multiplying the twenty barley loaves for a hundred men in 2 Kings 4:42–44. There is in all three stories the initial assessment of how much food is available, the prophetic command to divide it among a hopelessly large number, the skeptical objection, puzzled obedience, and the astonishing climax in which not only all are fed, but they had leftovers as well. And, as Helms[36] notes, the servant of Elisha has become the boy whose five barley loaves Jesus uses to feed the crowd (John 6:9, "There is a lad here who has five barley loaves and two fish").

In all this, my point has been to show, not how the New Testament evangelists rewrote and reapplied these Old Testament stories to Jesus, but rather how the episodes may be naturally read as mimetic reproductions of the ancient Elijah (and Elisha) stories by those who understood Jesus to be the predicted return of Elijah. These materials, then, would be what is left of the pre-canonical gospel of Jesus-Elijah. We now find them in our New Testament repurposed by writers representing the belief that Jesus was much more than a new Elijah, namely the Christ, the Son of God. But in view of that very fact, the imitation of Elijah seems suddenly recognizable as incongruous with the canonical Christology and the scriptures dedicated to promoting it. The Elijah-like stories are pointing in a different direction. "Who do men say that I am?" "Some say Elijah."

---

36. Helms, *Gospel Fictions,* p. 76.

3

THE PROPHET LIKE MOSES

Throughout this study I am exploring the likelihood, as it seems to me, that the canonical gospels are not unitary, seamless garments like modern novels or treatises, but are instead analogous to living organisms containing "junk DNA" which sometimes manifests itself in puzzling vestigial features. Another analogy might be the classic ransom note left by a kidnapper, its message composed from individual words or even letters cut from divers magazine advertisements. The result makes sense but clearly reveals its origin from disparate sources. In this way we may recognize bits and pieces of various early Christological traditions occurring side by side on the same page of this or that gospel. As long as each appeared to glorify Jesus, in it went, consistency be damned. This renders futile the endeavor of conventional exegesis to formulate a single, systematic Christology for each gospel. The implausible, strained character of such attempts is then recognizable as ingenious but contrived harmonization. I can think of no better example of this than the (unbelievably and tediously repetitive) works of Jack Dean Kingsbury,[37] who fashions a descending pyramid of Christologies and sub-Christologies, patching in this and that Christological title at appropriate places. Sometimes the result is

---

37. Jack Dean Kingsbury, *The Christology of Mark's Gospel* (Philadelphia: Fortress Press, 1983); Kingsbury, *Matthew: Structure, Christology, Kingdom* (Philadelphia: Fortress Press, 1975).

as if someone used pieces from two or three jigsaw puzzles, assuming they all belonged together, and wound up fashioning an ingenious but incoherent puzzle made of ill-fitting, bent fragments with shapeless gaps between them. For instance, Kingsbury[38] is hell-bent on synthesizing a Markan Christology of Jesus as the "royal Son of God," the Scion of David—despite Mark 12:35–37 directly refuting Davidic descent of the Messiah.[39] No, er, ah, Jesus just meant the Christ is, uh, the son of David *and then some*. Yeah, that's the ticket!

Does Mark actually say that some (whether in Jesus' day or his own) believed Jesus was "the Prophet like Moses" (Deut. 18:15, 18)? In Mark 6:15 and 8:28 we read that some deemed him "one of the prophets of old." But which one? Surely Moses, as John knows when his version (John 1:21) changes this to "Are you the Prophet?" That is, the expected Prophet like Moses, whom to reject means excommunication from the people of God (Acts 3:23; Deut. 18:19 plus Lev. 23:29). After all, who else could people have in mind? Obadiah? Nahum? Gad? Not likely. Plus the fact that, as Terence Collins demonstrates,[40] the so-called Writing Prophets are essentially literary characters (even if based on real charismatics) modeled upon the Moses character. Also remember how John 4:25–26 has the Samaritan woman, eager to change the subject as Jesus is beginning to get a bit too personal, mentions the coming Mosaic Taheb (for that was the Samaritan Messiah analog), and Jesus says that's who he is! In plain terms, he is the predicted Prophet like Moses.

Moses in a Manger

It is no secret that the Nativity of Jesus as found in Matthew's gos-

---

38. Kingsbury. *Mark,* p. 66.

39. Kingsbury. *Mark,* pp. 109–111.

40. Terence Collins, *The Mantle of Elijah: The Redaction Criticism of the Prophetical Books.* The Biblical Seminar (Sheffield: JSOT Press, 1993), p. 141.

pel is simply paraphrased from Josephus' birth narrative of Moses, which is in turn a rewrite of the one in the beginning of Exodus. This is plain from the occurrence in Matthew of elements absent from Exodus but added by Josephus.[41]

I am suggesting that Matthew appropriated this Mosaic Jesus birth narrative from a previous source stemming from the sect whose members understood Jesus to be, not the Davidic Messiah, but rather the Prophet like Moses. In fact, who else *would* have written it? We have become blind to the obvious. If you spend this much time making Jesus look like Moses, you must view Jesus as the Prophet like Moses. If that was *not* your intent, you have given your readers a bum steer.

None of my Business

Approached by someone in the crowd who seeks to have him adjudicate an inheritance dispute, Jesus refuses to play the role of arbiter, one commonly played by itinerant Near Eastern holy men (who, having no earthly connections or interests, the theory went, must be impartial as well as inspired). His retort, "Man, who made *me* a judge or divider over you?" (Luke 12:14), echoes and no doubt derives from Exodus 2:14a, "Who made *you* a prince and a judge over us?" Moses had sought to interfere in his people's worldly troubles, only to be rebuffed. By contrast, Jesus' intervention is sought, but he rebuffs the request. Here is another Moses-Jesus antitype, this time at the expense of Moses, since one greater than Moses, i.e., like Moses only better, is ostensibly here. As we shall soon see, Moses sat as judge, adjudicating disputes among his people all day long. We are to understand his activity as providing legal precedents eventually forming the basis for the

---

41. Once a parishioner of mine was giving a children's sermon about Moses and began to include bits of the Moses story that he assumed came from the Bible but actually stemmed from Josephus. He had picked them up from watching *The Ten Commandments* which was based on no less than three different once-popular Moses novels, one of which had derived extra material from Josephus and Philo.

Torah. But this tradition was eventually eclipsed by the Sinai sequence. Moses had functioned as an on-the-spot oracle, but this
version yielded to the more spectacular version in which Moses
received the commandments all at once in a lump sum literally
from the hand of Jehovah. I think this is why Luke felt free not to
depict Jesus settling cases like Judge Wapner on *People's Court*: the
Moses parallel was no longer relevant. Matthew (like his source)
simply associated Moses with the revelation on Sinai and so depicted Jesus issuing his commandments from another mountain
peak (hilltop?).

Sacred Sidekicks

> And passing along by the Sea of Galilee, he saw Simon and
> Andrew the brother of Simon casting a net in the sea; for they
> were fishermen. And Jesus said to them, "Follow me and I will
> make you become fishers of men." And immediately they left
> their nets and followed him. And going on a little farther, he
> saw James the son of Zebedee and John his brother, who were in
> their boat mending the nets. And immediately he called them;
> and they left their father Zebedee in the boat with the hired
> servants, and followed him. (Mark 1:16–20)

As Bowman suggests,[42] when Jesus summons James and John as
well as Peter and Andrew, two pairs of brothers, he is made to reenact Moses' recruitment of his own unsuspecting brother Aaron
at the analogous point in the Exodus story (4:27–28).

Sage Advice

We return to the tradition of Moses' stint as an oracular ombuds-
man. In Exodus chapter 18 Moses' father-in-law Jethro, himself
a hereditary priest and sage, visits Moses after the escape from
Pharaoh and Egypt. He has been taking care of his daughter, Moses' wife Zipporah, and their young children during the conflict.

---

42. Bowman, *The Gospel of Mark*, p. 157.

He is concerned when he observes how Moses, the sole source of divine guidance for his people, is close to burn-out, hearing cases from dawn to dusk without a break. He presumes to advise Moses to appoint lower court judges to deal with disputes by applying precedents Moses has already promulgated. That way, he can relax a bit, saving his energy for new and special problems. He will act as the Supreme Magistrate. Moses at once sees the wisdom of the plan.

> Jethro, the priest of Midian, Moses' father-in-law, heard of all that God had done for Moses and for Israel his people, how the LORD had brought Israel out of Egypt. Now Jethro, Moses' father-in-law, had taken Zipporah, Moses' wife, after he had sent her away, and her two sons, of whom the name of the one was Gershom (for he said, "I have been a sojourner in a foreign land"), and the name of the other, Eliezer (for he said, "The God of my father was my help, and delivered me from the sword of Pharaoh"). And Jethro, Moses' father-in-law, came with his sons and his wife to Moses in the wilderness where he was encamped at the mountain of God. And when one told Moses, "Lo, your father-in-law Jethro is coming to you with your wife and her two sons with her," Moses went out to meet his father-in-law, and did obeisance and kissed him; and they asked each other of their welfare, and went into the tent. Then Moses told his father-in-law all that the LORD had done to Pharaoh and to the Egyptians for Israel's sake, all the hardship that had come upon them in the way, and how the LORD had delivered them. And Jethro rejoiced for all the good which the LORD had done to Israel, in that he had delivered them out of the hand of the Egyptians. And Jethro said, "Blessed be the LORD, who has delivered you out of the hand of the Egyptians and out of the hand of Pharaoh. Now I know that the LORD is greater than all gods, because he delivered the people from under the hand of the Egyptians, when they dealt arrogantly with them." And Jethro, Moses' father-in-law, offered a burnt offering and sac-rifices to God; and Aaron came with all the elders of Israel to eat bread with Moses' father-in-law before God. On the mor-row Moses sat to judge the people, and the people stood about Moses from morning till evening. When Moses' father-in-law

saw all that he was doing for the people, he said, "What is this that you are doing for the people? Why do you sit alone, and all the people stand about you from morning till evening?" And Moses said to his father-in-law, "Because the people come to me to inquire of God; when they have a dispute, they come to me and I decide between a man and his neighbor, and I make them know the statutes of God and his decisions." Moses' father-in-law said to him, "What you are doing is not good. You and the people with you will wear yourselves out, for the thing is too heavy for you; you are not able to perform it alone. Listen now to my voice; I will give you counsel, and God be with you! You shall represent the people before God, and bring their cases to God; and you shall teach them the statutes and the decisions, and make them know the way in which they must walk and what they must do. Moreover choose able men from all the people, such as fear God, men who are trustworthy and who hate a bribe; and place such men over the people as rulers of thousands, of hundreds, of fifties, and of tens. And let them judge the people at all times; every great matter they shall bring to you, but any small matter they shall decide themselves; so it will be easier for you, and they will bear the burden with you. If you do this, and God so commands you, then you will be able to endure, and all this people also will go to their place in peace." So Moses gave heed to the voice of his father-in-law and did all that he had said. Moses chose able men out of all Israel, and made them heads over the people, rulers of thousands, of hundreds, of fifties, and of tens. And they judged the people at all times; hard cases they brought to Moses, but any small matter they decided themselves. Then Moses let his father-in-law depart, and he went his way to his own country.

Mark 3 tells a very similar story about Jesus, the crowds, and the choice of subordinates. The parallels are strikingly close, yet the structure is quite different, different to the point where it seems someone has broken the Moses story in two parts and reversed their order. In Exodus 18, the embassy of Moses' relatives arrives first, the pressures of Moses' job are described, and the solution of appointing assistants is proposed and adopted. In Mark 3, Jesus first appoints his subordinates on his own initiative just *before* his relatives arrive, concerned about the press of the crowds, keeping Jesus so busy that he cannot even find the time for a lunch break. Someone announced the arrival of his family, just as someone announced Moses' kin arriving. But, unlike Moses, Jesus rebuffs his relatives, refusing to give them audience, and even repudiating any connection with them!

And he went up into the hills, and called to him those whom he desired; and they came to him. And he appointed twelve, to be with him, and to be sent out to preach and have authority to cast out demons: Simon whom he surnamed Peter; James the son of Zebedee and John the brother of James, whom he surnamed Boanerges, that is, sons of thunder; Andrew, and Philip, and Bartholomew, and Matthew, and Thomas, and James the son of Alphaeus, and Thaddaeus, and Simon the Cananaean, and Judas Iscariot, who betrayed him. Then he went home; and the crowd came together again, so that they could not even eat. And when his family heard it, they went out to seize him, for people were saying, "He is beside himself." And the scribes who came down from Jerusalem said, "He is possessed by Beel-zebul, and by the prince of demons he casts out the demons." And he called them to him, and said to them in parables, "How can Satan cast out Satan? If a kingdom is divided against itself, that kingdom cannot stand. And if a house is divided against itself, that house will not be able to stand. And if Satan has risen up against himself and is divided, he cannot stand, but is coming to an end. But no one can enter a strong man's house and plunder his goods, unless he first binds the strong man; then indeed he may plunder his house. Truly, I say to you, all sins will be forgiven the sons of men, and whatever blasphemies they utter; but whoever blasphemes against the Holy Spirit never has forgiveness, but is guilty of an eternal sin"— for they had said, "He has an unclean spirit." And his mother and his brothers came; and standing outside they sent to him and called him. And a crowd was sitting about him; and they said to him, "Your mother and your brothers are outside, asking for you." And he replied, "Who are my mother and my brothers?" And looking around on those who sat about him, he said, "Here are my mother and my brothers! Whoever does the will of God is my brother, and sister, and mother."

We must imagine that, previous to Mark, someone who regarded Jesus as the Prophet like Moses had rewritten the story of Moses heeding Jethro's advice to name subordinates, resulting in a scene in which choosing the twelve disciples was the idea of the Holy Family of Jesus. Note the similarities between Mark 3 and Exodus 18. Just as Moses' father-in-law Jethro hears of Moses' successes and brings Moses' wife and sons to him (Exod. 18:1–5), so do the mother and brothers of Jesus hear reports and journey to meet Jesus (Mark 3:21). Moses is constantly surrounded by suppliants (18:13–18), just like Jesus (3:20). Just as Moses' arriving family is announced ("Lo, your father-in-law Jethro is coming to you with your wife and her two sons with her" 18:6), so is Jesus' ("Behold, your mother and your brothers are outside looking for you," 3:31–32). "Moses went out to meet his father-in-law, and bowed down and kissed him; and they asked each other of their welfare, and went into the tent" (Exod. 18:7). Originally we would have read of Jesus welcoming his family. And as Jethro voices his concern for the harried Moses, suggesting he share the burden with a number of helpers (18:21–22), so we would have read that James or Mary advised the choice of assistants "that they might be with him, and that he might send them out to preach" (Mark 3:14). And Jesus would only then have named the Twelve.

Mark, acting in the interest of a church-political agenda, has broken the story into two and reversed its halves so as to bring dishonor on the relatives of Jesus (representing a contemporary faction claiming their authority) and to take from them the credit for naming the Twelve (which is also why he emphasizes that Jesus "summoned those that he *himself* wanted," i.e., it was all his own idea. As the text now reads, Jesus chooses the disciples, and only subsequently do his interfering relatives arrive harboring doubts about his sanity, and he rebuffs them (Mark 3:33–35).

Jesus, however, does not, like Moses, choose seventy (though

Luke will restore this number, Luke 10:1), but only twelve, based on the choice of the twelve spies in Deuteronomy 1:23, "The thing seemed good to me, and I took twelve men of you, one man for each tribe."[43]

Giving the Finger of God

Sandwiched into the middle of this material is a controversy between Jesus and his scribal critics who allege that he performs his exorcisms only by virtue of being in league with Beel-zebul. Some manuscripts read "Beel-zebub," harking back to 2 Kings 1:2–3. "Beel-zebul" denotes "Lord of the House," i.e., of the world, a powerful patron of exorcists, while "Beel-zebub" means "Lord of the Flies," denoting an oracle, since the priests would hear a sound like buzzing, the voice of spirits telling the desired fortune. Jesus' reply to the charge seems to come from Isaiah 49:24.[44]

> Can the prey be taken from the mighty, or the captives of a tyrant be rescued? Surely thus says the LORD: Even the captives of the mighty shall be taken, and the prey of the tyrant be rescued, for I will contend with those who contend with you, and I will save your children.

and from 1 Samuel 2:25: "If a man sins against a man, God will mediate for him; but if a man sins against the LORD, who can intercede for him?"[45]

Matthew and Luke (hence the Q source) make an interesting addition to Jesus' response to the scribes. Luke's, as usual, is probably closer to the Q original: "If I by Beel-zebul cast out demons, by whom do your sons cast them out? Consequently, they shall be your judges. But if I cast out demons by the finger of God,

---

43. Miller, *Gospel of Mark as Midrash*, p. 117.

44. Rikki E. Watts, *Isaiah's New Exodus and Mark*. Wissenschaftliche Untersuchungen zum Neuen Testament 2. Reihe 88 (Tübingen: Mohr Siebeck, 1997), pp. 148–149.

45. Miller, *Gospel of Mark as Midrash*, p. 136.

then the kingdom of God has come upon you" (Luke 11:19–20). Compressed into these verses is an unmistakable midrash upon the Exodus story of Moses' miracle contest with the magicians of Pharaoh. Initially able to match Moses feat for feat, they prove incapable of copying the miracle of the gnats and warn Pharaoh to give in, since "This is the finger of God" and no mere sorcery like theirs (Exod. 8:19). The "sons" of the scribes correspond to the Egyptian magicians and can dispel the scribes' charge against Jesus if they would. The Q version, of course, originated in the circles of those for whom Jesus was the Prophet like Moses. If you held any of the other possible pre-Christologies, why on earth would you picture Jesus saying (and doing) things like this?

Wild, Wild Wilderness

We have seen how the 2 Kings tale of Elisha multiplying food for his apprentices was likely the basis for similar miracles of Jesus as the returned Elijah (Elisha himself, of course, being a kind of "returned Elijah" in his own right). But surely a Moses Christology is implied in the pair of wilderness feedings in Mark. The isolated settings in Mark (i.e., in the underlying source) reflects the clamoring of the hungry Israelites during their nomadic wanderings, and Moses' sometimes exasperated but miraculous provision of quails, manna, and water amid the inhospitable dunes of the Hijaz. Nor are these the only Jesus versions of the Moses desert traditions. Remember how, in Q, Jesus resists the devil's blandishments in the wilderness by citing three texts from Deuteronomy.

> And he humbled you and let you hunger and fed you with manna, which you did not know, nor did your fathers know; that he might make you know that man does not live by bread alone, but that man lives by everything that proceeds out of the mouth of the LORD. (Deuteronomy 8:3)

> "You shall not put the LORD your God to the test, as you tested him at Massah. (Deuteronomy 6:16)

> You shall fear the LORD your God, and him only shall you
> serve, and you shall cleave to him, and by his name you shall
> swear. (Deuteronomy 6:13 LXX)

All of these refer to trials of the people of Israel in the wilderness
(the manna, Massa, and idolatry), which they failed, but which
Jesus, embodying a new Israel, passes with flying colors.[46]

The Shining

Mark's version of Jesus' Transfiguration seems to have originally
been the story of a resurrection appearance[47] issuing in Jesus' assumption into heaven via the Shekinah glory cloud. Moses and
Elijah, who also rose alive into heaven,[48] albeit without either dying or resurrecting, would seem to be on the scene in order to
welcome and accompany him. Originally, all three would have
been engulfed in the glowing cloud, leaving the other trio, of Peter,
James, and John, eager to erect those three stupas. Just how transfigured did Jesus get? Mark says Jesus' clothes became dazzling
white, whiter than any launderer on earth could have bleached
them. The reference would seem to be to the resurrection body,
commonly symbolized as a white robe (e.g., Matt, 22:12; Rev.

---

46. By the way, I believe that the Temptation narrative was absent from
Q because absent from the Ur-Lukas, as Marcion's version attests. I think
that Polycarp of Smyrna, the Ecclesiastical Redactor responsible for sup-
plementing Marcion's shorter text, copied the Temptation sequence from
Matthew, who had derived it from the traditions of the Mosaic Jesus sect.

47. Rudolf Bultmann, *History of the Synoptic Tradition*. Trans. John
Marsh (New York: Harper & Row, 1968), pp. 230, 259–260.

48. The narrative of Moses' departure in Deuteronomy 34:5–6 is cagey.
It says that God saw to Moses' "burial," and that no one knows where
the corpse might be found. Some inferred that the text is telling us, in
circuitous language, that God "buried" him, i.e., secreted him away, still
alive, just like the Hidden Imam. This was certainly the inference drawn
by Philo, Josephus, John the Revelator (Rev. 11:6b) and (I think) the
author of Jude, verse 9.

7:14).[49] But the version that appears in Matthew's gospel is significantly different, though it is easy not to notice that. This time, not only Jesus' clothes but also his *face* is shining brilliantly. One thinks at once, as he is intended to, of the blinding visage of Moses as he emerges from the Tent of Meeting, having consulted Jehovah inside. Again, Jesus is plainly depicted as the Prophet like Moses. Was this Matthew's redaction of Mark? Or an alternative version he preferred? In any case, if your favorite Christology was, say, the Messianic Son of David or the Danielic Son of Man, I don't know why you would compose or include something like this.

Meet the New Law, Same as the Old Law

Kingsbury simply refuses to believe his lying eyes when he denies that Matthew's gospel is constructed around the five major blocs of teaching: the Sermon on the Mount (chapters 5–7), the Mission Charge (chapter 10), the Parables chapter (13), the Manual of Discipline (chapters 18–19), and the denunciation of the Pharisees plus the Olivet Discourse (chapters 23–26; the cramming together of two themes in the fifth section only underlines his determination to squeeze the whole thing into five divisions, no matter how snug the fit!). Nonsense, says Kingsbury! No, he contends, Matthew's gospel must be divvied up at two hinge points, 4:17, where Jesus' public ministry of teaching and healing is launched, and 16:2, where Jesus informs his men of his pre-ordained fate, inaugurating the Passion narrative.[50]

Why this embarrassing absurdity? I wonder if the ancient writer would have shared Kingsbury's predilection for a structure with a single focus? But suppose he *did*. It's a reasonable hypothesis. The implication is interesting. Perhaps Matthew's two-headed structure is the result of the evangelist combining two sources: a building, stage-by-stage narrative such as Kingsbury proposes, and

---

49. Joachim Jeremias, *The Parables of Jesus*. Trans. S.H. Hooke (New York: Scribners, 2nd rev. ed., 1972), pp. 188–189.

50. Kingsbury, *Matthew: Structure, Christology, Kingdom*, p. 36.

a Jesus Pentateuch consisting of the five great teaching sections. This latter would be a good example of a wider literary phenomenon at that time: the production of sectarian New Torahs including the Qumran Manual of Discipline and the Book of Jubilees.

As has been remarked since time immemorial, the five-fold teaching of Jesus begins with this Prophet like Moses perching atop a mountain to issue new divine commandments. Sectarian tensions are evident from the outset when Jesus is made to warn the hearer/reader to disregard the teaching of some rival Jesus-sect that Jesus' mission was to nullify the scriptures ("the Law and the Prophets," i.e., the Tanach). No, he has come to reinforce scripture's binding authority (Matt. 5:15–17). In the style of the Rabbis, he proceeds to build a protective hedge about the biblical commandments. You will never get close enough to the murder command to be in danger of breaking it if you nip your murderous anger in the bud (5:21–22b). You'll never get within breaking distance of the adultery command if you only have eyes for your missus (5:27–29). You don't need to fear breaking your vows if you never make any, and you won't even be asked to if you have a sterling reputation for honesty (5:33–37). The problem with rival Jewish factions is not their allegiance to the commandments but rather their failure to obey them (5:20): their hypocrisy is all that saves them from antinomianism! And anti-Torah Jesus sectarians are in for a nasty surprise on the Day of Judgment when the Pearly Gates slam shut in their faces (7:21–23)! Monastic severity prevails among the "brothers." Internecine disputes must be adjudicated by the sect's council, a guilty verdict resulting in excommunication and even consignment to hell fire (5:22)!

The brethren are assured that, having sacrificed all worldly wealth to the common treasury, they need not worry since God will provide all their needs (6:19–25). When circulating among the secular folk during visits to town, they dare not yield to the ever-present temptation to capitalize on their conspicuous piety by what we today call "virtue-signaling" (6:1–7; 16–18). Is not their whole cloistered way of life (5:14b) aimed at preventing such self-aggrandizing ostentation?

The second section deals with the duties and dangers of itinerant preaching by the brethren, ranging from the likelihood of persecution by the authorities (10:40–42) to door-to-door mendicant trick-or-treating, exactly the practice of Buddhist monks today.

The third sayings group is a collection of parables more or less parallel to Mark chapter 4. One of the parables that is explained in some detail (13:24–30, 37–43) is that of the Wheat and the Tares, which deals with the challenge of Pauline Christians who preach freedom from the Torah. One day they will get theirs.

The disciples ask why Jesus "teaches" in parables unintelligible to the common listeners. The answer, already anticipated back in 7:6, is that the esoteric truths cherished by the Moses/Jesus sect must be shielded from outsiders incapable of understanding it, and who will both blaspheme it and abuse those who propound it.

The fourth module is a concise Manual of Disciple governing life in the brotherhood. Topics covered include sensitivity in dealing with new postulants, rules governing divorce, more about mediating disputes within the community, consecrated celibacy, infant baptism,[51] and the requirement of voluntary poverty for those who have mastered the conventional commandments and are prepared to give all to join the monastic fellowship. Most of these concerns simply do not apply to your average church congregation, today or back then.

The fifth book of the Jesus Torah begins with a damning indictment of the leadership of the sect's rival faction, probably the Yavneh Sanhedrin, whose admitted authority the Mosaic Jesus sect's leaders covet. So as not to expand into a Hexateuch,[52] our document segues into the Little Apocalypse, probably an earlier

---

51. Oscar Cullmann, *Baptism in the New Testament*. Trans. J.K.S. Reid. Studies in Biblical Theology No. 1 (London: SCM Press, 1950), Appendix: "Traces of an Ancient Baptismal Formula in the New Testament," pp. 71–80.

52. "We shall Hex the Pentateuch, and slip you in neatly between Numbers and Deuteronomy!" Jerome Lawrence and Robert E. Lee, *Inherit the Wind* (New York: Bantam Books, 1963), p. 90.

version than appears in Mark.[53] It is hardly surprising to find an apocalypse associated with a radical Jewish sect.

To me, one question is obvious. Even unavoidable. What would such a large-scale chunk of material self-evidently painting Jesus in Mosaic colors be doing in a gospel advocating faith in Jesus as the Davidic Messiah? They're just not the same thing. It looks as if the compiler no longer understood the distinction. But whomever he borrowed the Mosaic Jesus material from knew the difference.

Deutero-Deuteronomy

The word "Deuteronomy" is Greek for "Second Law" and refers to the fictive setting of the book according to which Moses has to educate the new generation of Israelites in the Law of God. Hoping you won't notice the differences from earlier "Mosaic" law codes, the compiler is actually accrediting a new code to Moses. It's like Poor Richard's Almanac or Webster's Dictionary. The name of the original compiler has become the title of the text, though little remains in common between the new edition and the original. The central section of Luke (10:1–18:14) forms what might be called a "Deutero-Deuteronomy," using the Book of Deuteronomy as a topical pattern for a new "code" of sorts. It is particularly striking that Luke's material here in the central section follows the order of the corresponding topics from Deuteronomy.[54] Thus what we have is an alternative version of a new Torah, this time not a whole new Pentateuch such as we find in Matthew's gospel. But it makes the best sense to me to attribute both versions to those sectarians who understood Jesus as the Prophet like Moses.

---

53. Hermann Detering, "The Synoptic Apocalypse (Mark 13 par): A Document from the Time of Bar Kochba." *Journal of Higher Criticism* Vol. 7, no. 2, Fall 2000, pp. 161–210.

54. C.F. Evans, "The Central Section of St. Luke's Gospel," in D.E. Nineham, ed., *Studies in the Gospels: Essays in Memory of R.H. Lightfoot* (Oxford: Basil Blackwell, 1967) was the first to point this out.

Advance Men (Deut. 1:20–46; Luke 10:1–3, 17–20)

Just as Moses had chosen twelve spies to reconnoiter the land which stretched "*before your face*," sending them through the *cities* of the land of Canaan, so does Jesus send a second group, after the twelve, a group of seventy, whose number symbolizes the nations of the earth who are to be conquered, so to speak, with the gospel in the Acts of the Apostles. He sends them out "*before his face*" to every *city* he plans to visit (in Canaan, too, obviously). To match the image of the spies returning with samples of the fruit of the land (Deut. 1:25), Luke has placed here the Q saying (Luke 10:2// Matt. 9:37–38), "The harvest is plentiful, but the workers are few; therefore beg the Lord of the harvest to send out more workers into his harvest."

Soles and Souls (Deut. 2–3:22; Luke 10:4–16)

Just as Moses sent messengers to Kings Og of Bashan and Sihon of Heshbon with terms of peace, so does Jesus send his seventy out with the offer of blessing: "Peace be to this house." The Israelite messengers are rebuffed, and God punishes them by sending Israel to decimate them. Jesus warns that in case of rejection (which does not in fact occur in the subsequent narrative), the aloof cities will face divine judgment some time in the future. This mission charge material comes from Q (cf. Matt. 10). That it did not originate here, but was borrowed directly from Deuteronomy, is evident from the fact that the hypothetical doom of the unresponsive towns is compared with those of Tyre and Sidon, not of Bashan and Heshbon. Perhaps the compiler decided to use the Q material here because it uses the image of the missionaries "shaking the dust" (i.e., the contagion) of the village "from the soles of their feet" (Luke 10:10), matching the mention of "the sole of the foot" in Deuteronomy 2:5.

Lord of Heaven and Earth (Deut. 3:23–4:40; Luke 10:21–24)

"At that time" Moses prayed to God, like unto whom there is none "in heaven or on earth" (Deut. 2:23–24). In the saying found in both Luke 10:21–24 and Matthew 11:25–27, perhaps itself suggested originally by the Deuteronomy text, Jesus "at that time" praised his divine Father, "Lord of heaven and earth" (Luke 10:21). Jesus thanks God for revealing his wonders to "children," not to the ostensibly "wise." In some measure this reflects the wording of Deuteronomy 4:6, where Moses reminds his people to cherish the commandments as their *wisdom* and 4:9, where he bids them tell what they have seen to their *children*. The Deuteronomic recital of all the wonders their eyes have seen (4:3, 9, 34, 36) may have inspired the Q blessing of the disciples for having seen the saving acts the ancient prophets and kings did not live to witness (Luke 10:23–24). Only note the antitypological reversal of Deuteronomy: in the Jesus version Q it is the ancients who failed to see what their remote heirs did see.

Top Ten Commandments
(Deut. 5:1–33; 6:1–25; Luke 10:25–27)

These two chapters of Deuteronomy present both the Decalogue and the Shema (the great creedal declaration of Jewish monotheism). Luke presents but the tip of the iceberg when Jesus asks a scribe what he considers the gist of the Torah and the man replies with the Shema (adding Leviticus 19:18). This is to rewrite Mark 12:28–34, which did list some of the Ten Commandments, albeit loosely. Jesus' closing comment, "Do this and you will live," comes from Leviticus 18:5, "You shall therefore keep my statutes and my ordinances, by doing which a man shall live."

The Compassionate, the Merciful (Deut. 7:1–10; Luke 10:29–37)

Deuteronomy's stern charge to eradicate the heathen of Canaan without mercy (7:2) is here opposed by the parable of the Good Samaritan, in which the despised foreigner/heretic is filled with mercy (Luke 10:33) for a Jew victimized by thugs. This parable, like the narrative of the Samaritan leper (Luke 17:1–19), might be a clue that this Deutero-Deuteronomy stems from a Samaritan sect who regarded Jesus as the Taheb, the Prophet like Moses. In this case we can appreciate the satirical/polemical depiction of the priest and the Levite, functionaries of the *Jerusalem* Temple, which Samaritans despised as a heretical substitute for their own temple at Mount Gerizim.

Not by Bread Alone (Deut. 8:1–3; Luke 10:38–42)

The story of Mary and Martha is (or at least is used as) a commentary on Deuteronomy 8:3, "Man does not live by bread alone, but . . . by every word that proceeds from the mouth of the LORD." The anecdote opposes the contemplative Mary who hungers for Jesus' ("the Lord's") "words" with the harried Martha, whose preoccupation with domestic chores, especially cooking and serving, threatens to crowd out spiritual sustenance (cf. Deut. 8:11–14).

Father Knows Best (Deut. 8:4–20; Luke 11:1–13)

He was praying in a certain place, and when he ceased, one of his disciples said to him, "Lord, teach us to pray, as John taught his disciples." And he said to them, "When you pray, say: "Father, hallowed be thy name. Thy kingdom come. Give us each day our daily bread; and forgive us our sins, for we ourselves forgive every one who is indebted to us; and lead us not into temptation." And he said to them, "Which of you who has a friend will go to him at midnight and say to him, 'Friend, lend me three loaves; for a friend of mine has arrived on a journey, and I have nothing to set before him'; and he will answer from within, 'Do not bother me; the door is now shut, and my children are with me in bed; I cannot get up and give you anything'? I tell you, though he will not get up and give him anything because he is his friend, yet because of his importunity he will rise and give him whatever he needs. And I tell you, Ask, and it will be given you; seek, and you will find; knock, and it will be opened to you. For every one who asks receives, and he who seeks finds, and to him who knocks it will be opened. What father among you, if his son asks for a fish, will instead of a fish give him a serpent; or if he asks for an egg, will give him a scorpion? If you then, who are evil, know how to give good gifts to your children, how much more will the heavenly Father give the Holy Spirit to those who ask him!"

Deuteronomy compares the discipline meted out to Israel by God with the training a father gives his son, then reminds the reader of the fatherly provision of God for his children in the wilderness and promises security, prosperity, and sufficient food in their new land. This version of the Lord's Prayer shares the same general themes of fatherly provision and asking God to spare his children "the test," recalling the "tests" sent upon the people by God in the wilderness. Likewise, the material about God giving good gifts to his children (Luke 11:9–13) echoes the point of the Deuteronomy text, together with the parable of the Importunate Friend, which urges the seeker not to give up praying "How long, O Lord?"

The Bigger They Are . . . (Deut. 9:1–10:11; Luke 11:14–26)

On the eve of Israel's entrance into the land, Moses reviews their fathers' sorry history of rebellion, yet promises victory over stronger nations including the half-mythical Anakim, descended from a race of titans. Later haggadah made these Sons of Anak descendants of the miscegenation between the Sons of God understood as fallen angels and the daughters of men (Gen. 6:1–6). Thus it is no surprise to find a parallel between this text and the account of the Beel-zebul controversy, where Jesus exorcises demons (fallen angels?), despoiling Satan, the strong man, of his captives. According to the analogy, the poor hapless demoniacs are like the promised land of Canaan, while the demons possessing the wretches are like the Anakim holding the land until God casts them out because of their wickedness, even though like Satan their chief they are far stronger than any mere mortal.

As noted in the discussion of the Beel-zebul controversy (above), the comparison of Jesus with the "sons" of the Pharisees, with his own use of "the finger of God" to cast out demons, must derive from a midrash upon the Exodus contest between Moses and the priest-magicians of Pharaoh. But we find it here, at this particular point, because of the Deuteronomic reference to "the finger of God" writing the commandments upon the stone tables. The "strong man" element of both Markan and Q versions of the Beel-zebul episode also originated elsewhere, in Isaiah 49:24, but it seemed to fit the Deuteronomic reference to stronger nations here.

Lighting the Lamp (Deut. 10:12–11:32; Luke 11:27–36)

To Deuteronomy's exaltation of God as impartial to all, no respecter of persons, we find an anecdote showing that not even the mother of Jesus is higher in God's sight than the average faithful disciple. And corresponding to the warning for Israel not to repeat the sins of the Canaanites and so repeat their doom, is the material on how even ancient non-Israelites better appreciated the divine witness of their day than did Jesus' contemporaries. And finally the material about the eye being the lamp of the body recalls Deuteronomy 11:18's charge to cherish the commandments in one's heart and to place them as frontlets on one's forehead. Presumably, the unstated middle term of transition from the one image to the other was Psalm 19:8 ("the precepts of the LORD are right, rejoicing the heart; the commandment of the LORD is pure, enlightening the eyes") or perhaps Psalm 119:105 ("Your word is a lamp for my feet and a light for my path.").

Clean and Unclean (Deut. 12:1–16; Luke 11:37–12:12)

The substance of Deuteronomy 12:1–14's prohibition of sacrifice on the traditional high places and restriction of worship to the (Jerusalem) Temple, finds no real echo in our Deutero-Deuteronomy, which waits to apply roughly parallel material to Deuteronomy 12:15–16, which allows for the preparation and eating of meat as a purely secular process at home. To this corresponds the inability of the Pharisees to tell the real difference between clean and unclean. The connection is merely that of catchwords (particular words used, often fortuitously, in both passages, regardless of context or even denotation), as proves also to be the case when we notice that the phrase "the blood of all the prophets shed" just barely recalls the Deuteronomic phrase, "you shall not eat the blood; you shall pour it out upon the earth" (12:16).

Prosperity and Inheritance (Deut. 12:17–32; Luke 12:13–34)

The link here is tenuous and vague, but both passages treat of prosperity and providence, of the next generation, of sacrifice and consumption. The ensuing parable, Luke 12:16–21, seems to be based on Ecclesiastes/Qoheleth 6:1–2, "a man to whom God gives wealth, possessions, and honor, so that he lacks nothing of all he desires, yet God does not give him the opportunity to enjoy them, but a stranger enjoys them." See also Ecclesiastes/Qoheleth 2:18–21.

Truth or Consequences (Deut. 13:1–11; Luke 12:35–53)

Deuteronomy takes aim at false prophets, prophets of rival deities, warning Israel not to heed their seductions. It is God who has sent them, and not the deities whom they think themselves to speaking for. God is in this way testing Israel's fidelity. Matching this theme we find parable material based on the Markan Apocalypse (Mark 13:34–37). The parable has the departing master set tasks for his servants; hence they function as tests to prove how well they will perform. Connecting the parable with Deuteronomy, the church's job while their Lord is away in heaven is to remain faithful to his name as against the blandishments of other saviors and prophets (Luke 21:8).

Deuteronomy does not exempt even family members who may have fallen under the spell of forbidden gods (13:6–11); even so, and the corresponding Christian saying (Luke 51–53//Matt. 10:34–36) is based on an unacknowledged quotation of Micah 7:6, "for the son treats the father with contempt, the daughter rises up against her mother, the daughter-in-law against her mother-in-law; a man's enemies are men of his own household."

Judgment on this People
(Deut. 13:12–18; Luke 12:54–13:5)

Whole cities lapsing into pagan apostasy are to be eliminated, destroyed, Deuteronomy mandates, with nothing ever to be rebuilt on the desolation, so seriously does Israel's God take spiritual infidelity. No less gravely does Jesus take the lack of repentance on the part of Galileans and Jews. Past tragedies and atrocities will be seen as the mere beginning of the judgments to fall like the headsman's ax on an unrepentant people. Of course, Jesus "prophesies" long after the fact, referring to the bloody triumph of Rome in Galilee and Judea culminating in 73 CE.

The Third Year (Deut. 14:28; Luke 13:6–9)

Deuteronomy 14:28 stipulates as follows: "At the end of every three years you shall bring forth all the tithe of your produce in the same year, and lay it up within your towns." The corresponding text in Deutero-Deuteronomy reads:

> And he told this parable: "A man had a fig tree planted in his vineyard; and he came seeking fruit on it and found none. And

he said to the vinedresser, 'Lo, these three years I have come seeking fruit on this fig tree, and I find none. Cut it down; why should it use up the ground?' And he answered him, 'Let it alone, sir, this year also, till I dig about it and put on manure. And if it bears fruit next year, well and good; but if not, you can cut it down.'"

Deuteronomy 14 mandates a tithe of one's produce every three years. But the rewrite version uses the law as a springboard for a retrospective parable accounting for the Roman defeat of Judea and Galilee, continuing the discussion from the preceding pericopae. The people of God is like a barren fig tree which has disappointed its owner three years straight, yielding nothing to offer to God. The vinedresser pleads for an extra year's grace period before the fruitless tree should be uprooted. The point: don't say God didn't go the second mile before exacting judgment.

Release of the Bondslave
(Deut. 15:1–18; Luke 13:10–21)

Deuteronomy calls for the cancellation of debts in the seventh year, a kind of release from bondage, as well as freedom for bond-servants. The last case stipulated is that of the bondwoman (Deut. 15:17). From this last, the Jesus version has developed the story of a woman, a bondservant of Satan for eighteen years by virtue of a bent spine, being freed by Jesus.

Off to Jerusalem (Deut. 16:1–17; 17:7; Luke 13:22–35)

Deuteronomy commands thrice-yearly pilgrimage to the Jerusa-lem Temple, and Jesus declares nothing will deflect his inexorable three-day progress to Jerusalem to die there as a prophet must.

Righteous Judges; Remembering the Poor
(Deut. 16:18–20; 17:8–18; Luke 14:1–14)

The fit here is loose, but the connection is nonetheless evident. Deuteronomy is concerned with people accepting the oracular verdict of priests and judges, and with limiting the prerogatives of the king. The Jesus version is set in the house of a "ruler" and tells the story of the dropsical man to exalt Jesus' judgment over that of the scribes. The rest of the passage refers back to the preceding Deuteronomic text, 16:14, whose ranking of various guests invites a piece of table etiquette borrowed from Proverbs 25:6–7 ("Do not put yourself forward in the king's presence or stand in the place of the great; for it is better to be told, 'Come up here,' than to be put lower in the presence of the prince."). The specific inclusion of the widow and the sojourner in Deuteronomy 16:14 has inspired Jesus' admonition to invite the poor, the maimed, the blind, and the lame instead of one's friends and relatives. While the Jesus version, disinviting one's relatives and friends, may seem a more radical suggestion than Deuteronomy's inclusion of the poor alongside one's family, it actually tends toward minimizing the discomfort of the situation: one can bask in playing the benefactor to one's poor clients without having to embarrass one's fellow sophisticates with the crude manners of the poor at the same table (though in 1 Corinthians 11:18–22 we learn some "solved" the problem by segregating the two groups at the same event!).

Excoooze Me! (Deut. 20; Luke 14:15–35)

Commentators commonly note the similarity between the excuses offered by those invited to the Great Supper (Matt. 22:1–10// Luke 14:16–24), implicitly sneered at by the narrator, and those circumstances exempting an Israelite from serving in holy war in Deuteronomy 20: building a new house, planting a new vineyard, getting married. One can only suspect that the gospel version represents a tightening up of what were considered by an enthusiastic sect to be too lax standards, just as the divorce rules were tightened by Christians. (Those stricter standards, intolerant of excuse-making, were now seen to apply, no doubt, to the spiritual crusade of evangelism.)

The parable of the Great Supper is very likely an adaptation of the rabbinic story of the tax-collector Bar-Majan, who sought to climb socially by inviting the respectable rich to a great feast. All, refusing to fall for the ploy, begged off, whereupon the tax-collector decided to share the food with the poor that it not go to waste. This act of charity did win him a stately funeral but was not enough to mitigate his punishment in hell (Jerusalem Talmud, *Hagigah*, II, 77d).

Rights of the First-Born versus Wicked Sons
(Deut. 21:15–22:4; Luke 15)

Our Deutero-Deuteronomy leaves aside Deuteronomy 21:1–14, with its treatment of corpses and female captives. But the Deuteronomic treatment of sons and their inheritance in 21:15–21 has suggested the theme of the Jesus' parable, which combines the elements of division of property between a pair of sons, the possibility of favoring the wrong one, and the problem of a rebellious son who shames his family. The parable replaces the sternness of the original legal provision with an example of mercy. Here the rebellious son is accepted in love, not executed!

Deuteronomy 22:1–4 stipulates all manner of lost objects which must be returned if found, just as two parables, now found in Luke 15:3–7 and 8–10, provide examples of lost things zealously sought and found.

Masters, Slaves, Money, and Divorce
(Deut. 23:15–24:4; Luke 16:1–18)

Luke skips Deuteronomy 22:5–23:14, a catch-all.

Luke appears to have used the Deuteronomy 23 provision for

the welcoming of an escaped slave to live in one's midst as the basis for his parable of the Dishonest Steward, who must soon leave his master's employ and so manipulates his master's accounts as to assure he will be welcomed into his grateful clients' midst after his dismissal.

Our Second Deuteronomy has nothing particular to say concerning cult prostitutes ("priestitutes," one might call them) and vows, but the Deuteronomic discussion of debts and usury inspires the accusation of the Pharisees as "lovers of money." Greed like theirs is an "abomination" before God, a word he has borrowed from the same Deuteronomic passage's condemnation of a man remarrying his divorced wife after a second man has also divorced her. On the question of divorce, we find an odd juxtaposition of the Deuteronomic provision with the diametrically opposite Markan rejection of divorce, even while adding that the Torah cannot change!

Vindications (Deut. 24:6–25:3; Luke 16:19–18:8)

Inspired by Deuteronomy's injunctions concerning fair treatment of the poor, the parable of the Rich Man and Lazarus makes a classic and colorful lesson of it. It is probably based upon both the Egyptian Tale of the Two Brothers, where the postmortem fates of two men are disclosed as a lesson for the living, and the rabbinic parable of the tax-collector Bar-Majan (*Hagigah*, II, 77d), discussed just above.

The saying about the millstone (Luke 17:1–2/Matt. 8:6–7) matches the Deuteronomic mention of a millstone as the irreplaceable tool of one's trade (24:6), a mere catchword connection.

The provision for a leper's cure and certification (Deut. 24:8–9) prompts the creation of another pro-Samaritan story (with Deuteronomy 24:14's counsel to treat the sojourning foreigner fairly also in mind). It is the story of the nine Jewish lepers whom Jesus cures without thanks versus the single Samaritan who returns to thank Jesus.

Deuteronomy 24:17–18, 25:1–3 is concerned with fair judgments rendered on behalf of the poor and fair treatment of widows. The creator of the Jesus version required no more inspiration than this to create his parable of the Unjust Judge who delays vindicating a widow too poor to bribe him till she finally wears him out. The point is to advocate patience in prayer: if even a corrupt judge will at length give in to a just petition, cannot the righteous God be expected to answer just prayers in his own time?

Patting Yourself on the Back (Deut. 26; Luke 18:9–14)

Deuteronomy provides a ritual confession, not of sin, but of obedient righteousness.

> When you have finished paying all the tithe of your produce in the third year, which is the year of tithing, giving it to the Levite, the sojourner, the fatherless, and the widow, that they may eat within your towns and be filled, then you shall say before the LORD your God, "I have removed the sacred portion out of my house, and moreover I have given it to the Levite, the sojourner, the fatherless, and the widow, according to all thy commandment which thou hast commanded me; I have not transgressed any of thy commandments, neither have I forgotten them; I have not eaten of the tithe while I was mourning, or removed any of it while I was unclean, or offered any of it to the dead; I have obeyed the voice of the LORD my God, I have done according to all that thou hast commanded me. Look down from thy holy habitation, from heaven, and bless thy people Israel and the ground which thou hast given us, as thou didst swear to our fathers, a land flowing with milk and honey."

But once again, the new Moses, Jesus, is better than the old Moses. What the first Lawgiver commanded, the second Moses lampoons as self-righteous puffery!

> He also told this parable to some who trusted in themselves that they were righteous and despised others: "Two men went up

into the temple to pray, one a Pharisee and the other a tax collector. The Pharisee stood and prayed thus with himself, 'God, I thank thee that I am not like other men, extortioners, unjust, adulterers, or even like this tax collector. I fast twice a week, I give tithes of all that I get.' But the tax collector, standing far off, would not even lift up his eyes to heaven, but beat his breast, saying, 'God, be merciful to me a sinner!' I tell you, this man went down to his house justified rather than the other; for every one who exalts himself will be humbled, but he who humbles himself will be exalted."

Let me reiterate: no one would take this kind of trouble if their Christology were other than that of the Prophet like Moses. It seems natural for Christians thousands of years later to "crown him with many crowns," heaping every possible honorific on our beloved Jesus. But I think this is anachronistic and even theologically inflationary. "Oh yeah, he's also the Prophet like Moses." It's merely one of many predicates, like the epithets of Superman: the Man of Steel, the Man of Tomorrow, the Last Son of Krypton, the Man of Might, the Metropolis Marvel, the Action Ace, etc., The sheer number of them trivializes any single one of them.

4

THE DIVINE HERO

A number of scholars have noted the gospels' similarity to, and probable dependence upon, the aretalogy ("story of virtue"),[55] though it remains controversial. The debate centers on the concept of the *theios aner*, or "divine man," a widespread character type in ancient Hellenistic religious biographies.[56] The pioneer work on the divine man was a seminal essay by Clyde Weber Votaw, *The Gospels and Contemporary Biographies in the Greco-Roman World*.[57] These were narratives relating the wise words and wondrous deeds of half-legendary figures including Pythagoras, Apollonius of Tyana, Alexander the Great, and Moses. Some were called "sons of God" or of this or that god. Apollonius was the incarnation of Proteus, Pythagoras the son of Apollo, Alexander the son of Zeus-Amon, etc. These divine pedigrees may have been figurative since the narrators sometimes explain that their heroes' power is a function of their being filled with divine wisdom, not quite the

---

55. Pretty much equivalent in meaning to the title of the lost Hebrew work cited in Joshua 10:13 and 2 Samuel 1:18, *The Book of Jashar*, or "Book of the Just."

56. Theodore J. Weeden, *Mark: Traditions in Conflict* (Philadelphia: Fortress Press, 1971), p. 55.

57. Clyde Weber Votaw, *The Gospels and Contemporary Biographies in the Greco-Roman World*. Facet Books. Biblical Series 27 (1915; rpt. Philadelphia: Fortress Press, 1970).

same thing. But the divine patronymics may as easily have been intended literally, given the similarity to the Hindu-Buddhist concept of the *siddhis*, or "perfections," supernormal powers including flight, water-walking, bi-location, super speed, etc.[58] Reading the various aretalogies, like Philostratus' *Life of Apollonius of Tyana*, one is constantly reminded of the gospels.

The Amazing Jesus

David Litwa[59] seeks to demonstrate the extent to which all major elements of the New Testament portrayal and conception of Jesus Christ are typical for contemporary analogous figures: Asclepius, Romulus, Hercules, Aristaeus, Apollonius of Tyana, Augustus Caesar, Dionysus, Enoch, Elijah, Moses and the rest. Litwa quotes fulsomely from Greco-Roman and Jewish sources about divine and deified immortals, whether legendary or ostensibly historical. These characteristic features include divine parentage/miraculous conception, heavenly pre-existence, benefactions to mankind, spectacular epiphanies to disciples, signaled by blinding light, numinous terror, and solemn declamations. There are transfigurations during the god's earthly sojourn and immortalizing deifications, sometimes after death, sometime instead of physical death, but in either case attested by the absence of any physical remains. The transfigured bodies of these divine figures possess physical substance but have sloughed off the impediments and infirmities of the flesh.

I would describe Litwa's book *Iesus Deus* as a much-augmented vindication of Charles H. Talbert's 1977 (so hated by Christian apologists) book *What Is a Gospel?* Like his predecessor, Litwa

---

58. Mircea Eliade, *Yoga, Immortality and Freedom*. Trans. Willard R. Trask. Bollingen Series LVI (Princeton: Princeton University Press, 1969), pp. 85–95. "And, perhaps more than any other civilization, India has always lived under the sign of 'men-gods'" (p. 95). And I'd say that's even better than a "divine man" Ideal Type.

59. M. David Litwa, *Iesus Deus: The Early Christian Depiction of Jesus as a Mediterranean God* (Minneapolis: Fortress Press, 2014).

makes quite clear that, as Justin, Tertullian, and others admitted, the ancient man in the street would recognize that, as Mary Magdalene put it, "in very many ways he's just one more." What it all points to, in my opinion, is that it is outrageous special pleading for apologists to pick out divine miracle-worker Jesus as unique in his historical reality. For years I have summed it up like this: if you admitted that superheroes like Captain Marvel (Shazam), the Martian Manhunter, Icon, and the Sentry are mere fictive figments, why would you insist that Superman really existed, really leaped tall buildings in a single bound, and really ran faster than a locomotive? As I say, Dr. Litwa is too polite to say it, so I will. Somebody has to.

A major point Litwa makes is to remind scholars to take seriously what Martin Hengel (who appears to have forgotten his discovery five minutes after he made it) long ago demonstrated (in his great book *Judaism and Hellenism*): long before the New Testament, Judea and Judaism had been thoroughly permeated with post-Alexander Hellenism. Classic marks of Judaism as we know it were absorbed from Hellenism, including the very institution of the Rabbinate (a sage with a circle of disciples), allegorical scripture exegesis, Stoic morality and the primacy of reason, belief in reincarnation, etc.

The problem Litwa bemoans is the vestigial invocation of the pre-Hengel portrayal of Judaism and Hellenism as separated by a chasm, Judaism as Abraham's bosom, separated by a vast gulf from the Hades of pagan Hellenism. Conservatives like to insist that early (i.e., Jewish) Christians would never have stooped to borrow the religious categories and mythemes of the uncircumcised! Oh no! So if Jesus looks suspiciously like pagan saviors and god-men it must be because Jesus was the real thing and pagans did their best to Xerox him—even centuries BCE! You see, the devil overheard the prophecies of Jesus given to Isaiah and his colleagues and fabricated cheap knock-offs of Jesus like Osiris, Attis, and the Martian Manhunter.

The same fallacy allowed scholars like Raymond E. Brown

and apologists like N.T. Wright, as Litwa cannily observes, to use Judaism as a buffer against paganism, i.e., to protect Christianity's "uniqueness" from the theologically distasteful prospect of pagan religious influences. Does John's gospel sound a lot like Gnosticism? Well, yes, but John also sounds like the Dead Sea Scrolls, written by pagan-hating Jews. So we should reject Gnosticism in favor of Essenism as an influence on John. Whew! Close one! Any available, possible Jewish parallel was to be automatically preferred to any posited non-Jewish source. Why? Because "we" want to keep the bloodline of Christianity pure. At bottom was the old anxiety to defend the supracesessionist claim that Christianity is the true heir of Old Testament scripture and religion.

On the other hand, critical scholars from Harnack to Bultmann believed that, contra Father Abraham's reply to Dives, it *was* possible to span the gap: Lazarus *did* manage to cross the great divide to bring Dives a paper cup of water. In other words, history-of-religions scholars (the *Religionsgeschichtliche Schule*) traced out commonalities between Jewish-Christian myths and doctrines and those of their competitors, and inferred, not unreasonably, that the biblical religions liked what they saw for sale on the shelves of paganism, and/or that converts from pagan religions to Judaism and Christianity did not, so to speak, put away their idols upon conversion but mixed them into their new religion, the very same sort of syncretism we see in indigenous Third-World churches today. It is no surprise that Harnack, who wanted to strip away the Hellenizing "husk" of Catholic Christianity to return to the supposed "kernel" of Jesus' gospel of universalizing religious humanism, also endorsed Marcion's call to jettison the uncomfortably Jewish Old Testament.

But would any of this intentional borrowing ("cultural appropriation") have been necessary if Christianity was born into a Mediterranean cultural matrix of broadly shared mythico-religious ways of thinking and believing? Litwa says no. Not that such syncretism could not have happened in individual cases, but Litwa shows the various religious communities were pretty much breathing the same air.

And at this point I cannot help comparing the whole scenario to that of longstanding but now collapsing assumptions about the supposed relation of Old Testament Hebrew religion and "Canaanite" paganism. For centuries, even within the Old Testament itself, it was taught that pure Torah-monotheism was the creed of Moses, though again and again Israel found itself succumbing to the temptation to adopt idolatrous and depraved elements of the neighboring Canaanite religions of Baal, Rimmon, Dagon, and Melkart. The efforts of reformer prophets, we read, were never totally successful or long-lasting. But recent rethinking and rereading have thrown all this over. It now seems clear that Jewish aniconic monotheism was a very late and spotty development, the more-or-less successful work of the Deuteronomic Reform (which I date to Hasmonean times). The Deuteronomists and their successors cooked up the notion of the recurring pollution of pure Israelite faith with paganism, idolatry, sex-magic, and polytheism as a cover for the fact that, for most of biblical "history," Israelite religion was at least half-pagan. How *could* it have been if Abraham and Moses established (Deuteronomic) monotheism at the very beginning? Yeah, it was the insidious influence of those darn Canaanites! Now we know, however, that the ancient Israelites simply *were* "Canaanites," just like their adjacent kinfolk (even the Pentateuch admits the fact) the Edomites, Ishmaelites, Ammonites, Moabites, Trilobites, etc. Their religions and pantheons were no more than local variations of each other. It was only in revisionist retrospect that the Deuteronomists distinguished between "the people of the land" and the children of Israel who displaced them. The abhorrent Canaanites of the Pentateuch, with their pagan ways, were simply the (caricatured?) ancestors of the later Jews themselves. In Ezra's and Nehemiah's time, the Deuteronomist party still called those who rejected their new creed "the people of the land," i.e., Canaanite pagans.

In precisely the same way, I think, both the proponents of the Christian syncretism model and the apologists who claim that pagans borrowed Christian beliefs operated on the false assumption of two originally distinct religions which did or did not influence one another. Sealing off one religious tradition from the other (Canaanite paganism versus Mosaic Monotheism; Judaism versus Hellenism) was a polemical tactic allowing scholars and apologists to reject what they didn't like and to retain what they did like, and to retroject the latter into the imagined past, creating a usable "holy history" legitimating their own favorite theology. But Litwa has made it clear that early Christians, Jews, and pagans were simply ladling out the same soup, though they might sprinkle different seasonings into it.

Divine Men and Ideal Types

So whence the dispute? Jack Dean Kingsbury[60] and others resist the idea that the gospel genre is part and parcel of this larger Hellenistic "divine man" genre. It is the uneasy conscience of the apologist, "the anxiety of influence," the defensive disinclination to admit that the Christian gospel is a creation of culture, of human imagination. "Flesh and blood have not revealed it unto thee, but my Father in heaven." The favorite evasion is to claim that "the differences outweigh the similarities" between the gospels and their analogues, or that the supposed category into which the gospels fit does not actually exist but is instead an artificial synthesis of elements not naturally fitting together. In this case, the gripe is that the proposed examples of "divine men" are not sufficiently similar to constitute a type to which the figures of Moses, Pythagoras, or (God forbid!) Jesus may be assigned. The same tactic is often employed to deny that there was any such thing as Gnosticism, or Mystery Religions, or dying-and-rising gods, or apocalypses, in short, anything that might seem to threaten Christian uniqueness. The operative principle, or perhaps anti-principle, is to ignore the concept of the Ideal Type. This is an admittedly artificial category

---

60. Kingsbury, *Christology of Mark's Gospel*, pp. 43–44.

in that it is a kind of textbook definition to which actual phenomena may or may not conform in every detail. They will not match each other at every point. It is *expected* that "the differences will be greater than the similarities." The Ideal Type collects the features the various phenomena do have in common in order to use it as a measuring stick against which to measure and explain the differences between the actual phenomena.

For instance, scholars labor to construct a viable list of criteria for classifying something as a religion (rather than, say, a philosophy or magic). But darned if they can come up with a list of features occurring in every phenomenon we tend to think of as a religion. Hmmm ... Theravada Buddhism has a doctrine of the human predicament, a doctrine of salvation, ritual prescriptions, etc., but, alas, no God concept. What, is Theravada then not a religion? That can't be right! Nor is it. The fact that Theravada lacks a God concept is a major clue as to the distinctive character of it *as* a religion. Theravada does not need a God, actually needs *not* to have a God because salvation is via self-reliance to a unique degree.

Or think of the miracle story paradigm: on the whole, miracle stories, whether Hellenistic, biblical, Buddhist, whatever, tend to follow a basic outline: scene setting, entrance of the miracle-worker, predicament/case history, hero's announcement of intent to solve the problem, skepticism of the bystanders, word or gesture of power, resolution, proof of it, acclaim of the crowd.[61] This is the *syntagmic* axis, the plot logic. The *paradigmatic* axis is the "drop-down menu" of options. What is the nature of the problem? Bereavement, sickness, danger at sea, starvation? Who needs help? Disciples, children, lepers, crowds in the wilderness? What does the hero do? Take the sufferer's hand? Stretch out his body over the sufferer's? Utter an incantation? Lay on hands? What's the proof? The raised person eats, showing he is no ghost. The demon,

---

61. Bultmann, *History of the Synoptic Tradition*, pp. 221–225; Gerd Theissen, *The Miracle Stories of the Early Christian Tradition*. Trans. Francis McDonagh (Philadelphia: Fortress Press, 1983), pp. 47–85.

though invisible to the eye, knocks over a bowl of water or panics pigs into stampeding. The ex-leper is certified as healed after a priestly inspection. But there is a standard skeleton for the story-teller to pack the preferred meat on. It may be that some of the filled blanks occur in a slightly different order (because of flash-backs, etc.), and some may not occur at all. But one has no trouble recognizing the story as a miracle story, thanks to the Ideal Type to which it largely conforms. Not every element appears in every case, but the basic pattern is remarkably consistent.

This is why a particular theological system, like the Kabbal-ah of Isaac Luria, which lacks cosmogonic dualism, may yet be classified as "Gnostic."[62] This is why Mithraism, the Isis cult, the religion of Attis, that of Dionysus, and of Eleusis all count as Mys-tery Religions, though some of their deities were not resurrected gods. And so on. But Kingsbury is eager to debunk the notion of a divine man because he wants to make room for his own prefer-ence. For him, Mark's Jesus is primarily and predominantly "God's Royal Son," though the term certainly occurs far more often in Kingsbury's book[63] than it does in Mark's.

It is patently obvious to more casual readers of the gospels, should they chance to learn of the divine man category, that Jesus fits right in. It is easier for them than for someone like Kingsbury because they are seeing the whole forest, while he is examining it tree by tree (and chopping down the ones that stand in his way). Before illustrating how closely Jesus matches the divine man para-digm, I want to widen the scope of it, as it leads right into the larg-er Mythic Hero Archetype. The major recurring features of it as compiled by Lord Raglan, Otto Rank, and Alan Dundes[64] include

62. Gershom G. Scholem, *Jewish Gnosticism, Merkabah Mysticism, and Talmudic Tradition*. Based on the Israel Goldstein Lectures, delivered at the Jewish Theological Seminary of America, New York (New York: Jew-ish Theological Seminary of America, 1965).

63. Kingsbury, *Christology of Mark's Gospel*, pp. 66, 68, 69, 70, 71, 73, 75, 76, 77, 78, 88, 89, 100, 102.

64. Otto Rank, Lord Raglan, and Alan Dundes, *In Quest of the Hero*. Mythos: the Princeton/Bollingen Series (Princeton: Princeton University

a divine annunciation, a miraculous conception, omens announcing the hero's birth, his royal lineage, a child prodigy episode, temptation by a devil, performing miracles, being proclaimed king but eventually rejected, put to death on a hilltop, a mystery about his burial place, his postmortem farewell, and his assumption into heaven. Many or most of these motifs occur in the hagiographies of heroes, saints, and founders such as Oedipus, Prince Siddhartha, King Arthur, Hercules, etc., etc.

Jesus' virginal conception is announced by angels to both Mary and Joseph. At the predicted birth, angels and stars herald the event. Despite the humble circumstances of his birth, Jesus is of royal descent. Like his counterparts Zoroaster, Krishna, Octavian, and Moses, he survives attempts by wicked forces to eliminate the Holy Child. While a callow youth, he nonetheless shows himself to be a prodigy possessing wisdom beyond that of his would-be teachers. Like Prince Siddhartha, Abraham, and Zoroaster, Jesus rejects the temptations of the Evil One to seduce him from his mission. He does countless miracles. His popular acclaim leads to his (symbolic) installation as king (on Palm Sunday), though just as quickly the crowds turn on him, leading to his crucifixion on the hill of Golgotha. There is confusion among his mourners as to where to find his body. He then appears mysteriously, like Apollonius and Romulus, to bid them farewell before rising bodily into the heavens. That's pretty much the whole package right there! All this is well known, though seldom discussed by conservative apologists.

Romantically Involved

But virtually never mentioned is the striking fact that the gospels also match certain features often found in a related ancient genre, the ancient romance novels. This should not surprise us, since these genres (like all genres) are not air-tight. The ancient romances and

Press, 1990).

the aretalogies tend to shade over into one another. For example, *The Alexander Romance* and Philostratus' *Life of Apollonius of Tyana* have equal elements of both types. In the present chapter, the similarity of the gospels to the ancient novels will take on striking relevance. For their plot-devices mirror at crucial points some of the gospel episodes considered by almost all scholars of whatever theological stripe to be bedrock history.

Three major plot devices recur like clockwork in the ancient novels, which were usually about the adventures of star-crossed lovers, somewhat like soap operas today. First, the heroine, a princess, collapses into a coma and is taken for dead. Prematurely buried, she awakens later in the darkness of the tomb. Ironically, she is discovered in the nick of time by grave robbers who have broken into the opulent tomb, looking for rich funerary tokens (like King Tut's treasure-lined tomb, which is why most of the Pyramid tombs were empty by the time archaeologists got to them). The crooks save her life but also kidnap her, since they can't afford to leave a witness behind. When her fiancé (or husband) comes to the tomb to mourn, he is stunned to find the tomb empty and initially guesses that his beloved has been taken up to heaven by the gods who envied her beauty. In one tale, the man sees the shroud left behind, just as in John 20:6–7.

The second stock plot device is that the hero, finally realizing what has happened, goes in search of the heroine and eventually runs afoul of a governor or king who wants her and, to get him out of the way, has the hero crucified. Of course, the hero always manages to get a last minute pardon, even once affixed to the cross, or he survives crucifixion by some stroke of luck. Sometimes the heroine, too, appears (again!) to have been killed but winds up alive after all.

Third, we eventually have a joyous reunion of the two lovers, each of whom has despaired of ever seeing the other again. They at first cannot believe they are not seeing a ghost come to comfort them. Finally they are convinced that their loved one has survived in the flesh. Anyone who professes not to see major similarities between these novels, long ignored by scholars because of their supposed frivolity, and the gospels either has never read the gospels or does not want to admit the disturbing parallels.

Crosses and Tombs

In Chariton's *Chaereas and Callirhoe*, Chaereas, falsely incited to fury at his wife Callirhoe, gives her a powerful kick, seemingly killing her. She is then the victim of a Poe-esque premature burial. Soon some pirates (a prop pretty much ubiquitous in these novels) appear, planning to rob the tomb. They are startled to find Callirhoe alive, revived by the cool air of the tomb. Not eager to add murder to their crimes, they kidnap her instead, to sell her as a slave. While enduring her captivity, Callirhoe pities herself less than her bereaved husband in terms recalling the empty tomb narratives of the gospels: "You are mourning for me and repenting and sitting by an empty tomb. . . ."[65] The resemblance to the gospels only grows stronger once poor Chaereas discovers the empty tomb.

> When he reached the tomb, he found that the stones had been moved and the entrance was open. He was astonished at the sight and overcome by fearful perplexity at what had happened. Rumor—a swift messenger—told the Syracusans this amazing news. They all quickly crowded round the tomb, but no one dared go inside until Hermocrates gave an order to do so. The man who went in reported the whole situation accurately. It seemed incredible that even the corpse was not lying there. Then Chaereas himself determined to go in, in his desire to see Callirhoe again even dead; but though he hunted through the tomb, he could find nothing. Many people could not believe it and went in after him. They were all seized by helplessness. One of those standing there said, "The funeral offerings have been carried off [Cartlidge's translation reads: "The shroud has been stripped off"—cf. John 20:6–7]—it is tomb robbers who

---

65. Trans. B.P. Reardon, ed., *Collected Ancient Greek Novels* (Berkeley: University of California Press, 1989), p. 37.

have done that; but what about the corpse—where is it?" Many different suggestions circulated in the crowd. Chaereas looked towards the heavens, stretched up his arms, and cried: "Which of the gods is it, then, who has become my rival in love and carried off Callirhoe and is now keeping her with him . . . ?"[66]

The parallels to the empty tomb accounts, especially to John 20:1–10, are as abundant as they are close. Chaereas even suggests that Callirhoe has been (like Jesus) translated to heaven. We find an almost identical scene in Photius' summary of Iamblichus' otherwise lost *Babylonian Story*:

> The grave of the young woman is left empty, and there are left behind several robes that were to be burned on the grave, and food and drink. Rhodanes and his companion feast on the food and drink, take some of the clothing, and lie down to sleep in the young woman's grave. As daylight comes, those who set fire to the robber's house realize that they have been tricked and follow the footprints of Rhodanes and Sinonis, supposing that they are henchmen of the robber. They follow the footprints right up to the grave and look in at the motionless, sleeping, wine-sodden bodies lying in the grave. They suppose that they are looking at corpses and leave, puzzled that the tracks led there.[67]

Subsequently Callirhoe reflects on her misfortunes: "I have died and come to life again." (62). Later still, she laments, "I have died and been buried; I have been stolen from my tomb." Note the parallel to 1 Corinthians 15:3–4, "that Christ died . . . , that he was buried, that he was raised . . . " Scholars debate whether the "buried" reference in 1 Corinthians means to imply a tomb emptied by the resurrection. I would venture that the parallel with *Chaereas and Callirhoe* does suggest such an implication, since in the latter, disappearing from the tomb is equal to rising from the dead. Towards the end of the novel Callirhoe recounts "how she had come

66. Trans. Reardon, in Reardon, *Greek Novels*, p. 53.
67. Trans. Gerald N. Sandy, in Reardon, *Greek Novels*, p. 787. Cf. Luke 24:12.

back to life in the tomb."[68]

In Miletus Callirhoe comes to believe that Chaereas perished while searching for her. She has meanwhile married Dionysius. He wishes to console her and to provide closure, so the new husband erects a tomb for Chaereas. It lacks his body, not, as all believe, because no one knows the corpse's location, but because he is still alive elsewhere. In fact he is at that very moment being condemned to the cross!

> Without even seeing them or hearing their defense the master at once ordered the crucifixion of the sixteen men in the hut. They were brought out chained together at foot and neck, each carrying his cross. . . . Now Chaereas said nothing when he was led off with the others, but [his friend] Polycharmus, as he carried his cross, said: "Callirhoe, it is because of you that we are suffering like this! You are the cause of all our troubles!"[69]

Just in the nick of time Chaereas' sentence is commuted.

> Mithridates sent everybody off to reach Chaereas before he died. They found the rest nailed up on their crosses; Chaereas was just ascending his. So the executioner checked his gesture, and Chaereas climbed down from his cross.[70]

As he later recalls, "Mithridates at once ordered that I be taken down from the cross—I was practically finished by then." Here, then, is a hero who went to the cross for his beloved and returned alive. In the same story, a villain is likewise crucified, though, gaining his just deserts, he is not reprieved. This is Theron, the pirate who carried poor Callirhoe into slavery. "He was crucified in front of Callirhoe's tomb."[71] We find another instance of a crucifixion adjacent to the tomb of the righteous in *The Alexander Romance*

---

68. Reardon, in Reardon, *Greek Novels*, p. 111.

69. Reardon, in Reardon, *Greek Novels*, p. 67.

70. Reardon, in Reardon, *Greek Novels*, p. 69.

71. Reardon, in Reardon, *Greek Novels*, p. 57.

when Alexander arrests the assassins of his worthy foe Darius. He commanded them "to be crucified at Darius's grave."[72] We cannot help being reminded of the location of Jesus' burial "in the place where he was crucified" (John 19:41).

We meet with the familiar pattern again in the *Ephesian Tale* of Xenophon. It looks like beautiful Anthia has died from a dose of poison, but it has only placed her in a deathlike coma. She awakens from it in the tomb.

> Meanwhile some pirates had found that a girl had been given a sumptuous burial and that a great store of woman's finery was buried with her, and a great horde of gold and silver. After nightfall they came to the tomb, burst open the doors, came in and took away the finery, and saw that Anthia was still alive. They thought that this too would turn out very profitable for them, raised her up, and wanted to take her.[73]

Later on Habrocomes goes in search of her and eventually gets condemned to death through a long sequence of misadventures. "They set up the cross and attached him to it, tying his hands and feet tight with ropes; that is the way the Egyptians crucify. Then they went away and left him hanging there, thinking that the victim was securely in place." But Habrocomes prays that he may yet be spared such an undeserved death. He is heard for his loud cries and tears. "A sudden gust of wind arose and struck the cross, sweeping away the subsoil on the cliff where it had been fixed. Habrocomes fell into the torrent and was swept away; the water did him no harm; his fetters did not get in his way . . ."[74]

Finally Habrocomes returns to a temple where he and his beloved had once erected images of themselves, dedicating them (and thus themselves) to Aphrodite. Still without Anthia and supposing her to be dead, he sits there and weeps. He is found there

---

72. Trans. Ken Dowden, in Reardon, *Greek Novels*, p. 703.
73. Trans. Graham Anderson, in Reardon, *Greek Novels*, pp. 151–152.
74. Anderson, in Reardon, *Greek Novels*, p. 155.

by his old companions Leucon and Rhode.

> They did not recognize him, but wondered who would stay
> beside someone else's offerings. And so Leucon spoke to him.
> "Why are you sitting weeping, young man . . . ?" Habrocomes
> replied, "I am . . . the unfortunate Habrocomes!" When Leucon
> and Rhode heard this they were immediately dumfounded, but
> gradually recovered and recognized him by his appearance and
> voice, from what he said, and from his mention of Anthia.[75]

Who will not see here a striking resemblance to the New Testament empty tomb stories, where Jesus or an angel addresses a
weeping mourner, provoking a dramatic recognition? Remember
John 20:11–16, where we likewise have the question "Why are you
weeping?" the initial failure of recognition, then the recognition
sparked by the mention of a woman's name. Luke 24:13 ff. is very
nearly as close.

Achilles Tatius' *Leucippe and Clitophon* provides two harrowing scenes, worthy of a Saturday afternoon movie serial, in which
the heroine appears to be disemboweled. But it turns out to be
sleight-of-hand or mistaken identity. In the first Leucippe has to
recline in a coffin until her faked sacrifice. A confederate warns her
to "stay inside the coffin as long as it was daylight and not try to
come out even if she woke up early."[76] She eventually emerges alive
and well, giving us another "resurrection" scene. Later she relates
her adventure in a letter to Clitophon: "For your sake I have been
a sacrificial victim, an expiatory offering, and twice have died."[77]

Another character marvels over Leucippe's many "sham
deaths." "Hasn't she died many times before? Hasn't she often
been resurrected?"[78]

In another scene our heroine is required to prove her virginity
by means of an old ritual involving a syrinx instrument. If she has

75. Anderson, in Reardon, *Greek Novels*, p. 67.

76. Trans. John J. Winkler, in Reardon, *Greek Novels*, p. 220.

77. Winkler, in Reardon, *Greek Novels*, p. 242.

78. Winkler, in Reardon, *Greek Novels*, p. 262.

lied about her virginity, the syrinx is silent, and instead of music, a scream is heard from the cave. At once the populace quits that place, leaving the woman in the cave. On the third day a virgin priestess enters to find the syrinx lying on the ground, with no trace of the woman. It's the gospel truth: on the third day a woman comes to a cave in which someone was entombed but now finds no trace of a body! Sound familiar?

In Longus' *Daphnis and Chloe* we find only traces of the pattern, but they are worth noting anyway. "He ran down to the plain, threw his arms around Chloe, and fell down in a faint. . . . [H]e was, with difficulty, brought back to life by Chloe's kisses and the warmth of her embraces. . . ."[79] Later we hear that in the bleak midwinter Daphnis, deprived of the sight of his beloved Chloe, "waited for spring as if it were a rebirth from death."[80]

Later still, when vandals have despoiled the garden tended by happy pastoral folk, some anticipate harsh reprisal: "'There's an old man [the master will] string up on one of the pines, like Marsyas; and perhaps he'll . . . string up Daphnis, too!' . . . Chloe mourned . . . at the thought that Daphnis would be strung up . . . . When night was already falling, Eudromus brought them the news that the old master would arrive in three days' time. . . ,"[81] but all ends well.

The pattern comes into sharper focus again in Heliodorus' *Ethiopian Story*, where Knemon hides Charikleia, lover of Theagenes, in a cave for her safety.

> "Put her in, my friend, close the entrance with the stone in the normal way, and then come back . . . " this stone dropped effortlessly into place and could be opened just as easily. . . . Not a sound passed Charikleia's lips; this new misfortune was like a deathblow to her, separation from Theagenes tantamount to the loss of her own life. Leaving her numbed and silent, Knemon

---

79. Trans. Christopher Gill, in Reardon, *Greek Novels*, p. 315.

80. Gill, in Reardon, *Greek Novels*, p. 319.

81. Gill, in Reardon, *Greek Novels*, p. 336.

climbed out of the cave, and as he replaced the threshold stone, he shed a tear in sorrow for himself at the necessity that constrained him, and for her at the fate that afflicted her; he had virtually entombed her alive. . . .[82]

We find two additional episodes of apparent death and resurrection in *The Story of Apollonius, King of Tyre*. The king's wife appears to have died during childbirth while on a sea voyage, though the text baldly says, "she suddenly died."[83] They place her body in a sealed coffin and commit her to the sea. "Three days later waves cast up the coffin."[84] A medical student examines the body and discerns subtle signs of lingering life. He manages to reawaken her, though it is only some years later that her loved ones learn she is not dead after all.

The baby daughter grows up and is given into the care of foster parents by the grief-stricken Apollonius. Coveting her royal possessions, her wicked foster-mother schemes to have young Tarsia, for that is her name, assassinated. But in the event, the hired killer cannot bring himself to pull the trigger and secretly sells her into a brothel. Meanwhile, the foster-mother, thinking Tarsia dead, cooks up a false story of how she died and builds an "empty tomb"[85] to honor her memory. Tarsia resourcefully manages to maintain her virginity even in the midst of the brothel. One day she is hired to visit a despairing old man (Apollonius, of course) to cheer him up. This she tries to do with nothing more salacious than moral exhortations, bidding him to "come out of the darkness and into the light."[86]

Once the two recognize one another, he says, "my hope has been brought back to life."[87] When the townspeople learn of Tar-

---

82. Trans. J.R. Morgan, in Reardon, *Greek Novels*, p. 375.

83. Trans. Gerald N. Sandy, in Reardon, *Greek Novels*, p. 752.

84. Sandy, in Reardon, *Greek Novels*, p. 753.

85. Sandy, in Reardon, *Greek Novels*, p. 758.

86. Sandy, in Reardon, *Greek Novels*, p. 763.

87. Sandy, in Reardon, *Greek Novels*, p. 767.

sia's identity, they avenge the outrage perpetrated upon royalty, killing the pimp whose slave Tarsia was. Apollonius responds, "Thanks to you, death and grief have been shown to be false."[88] Once he has also been reunited with his wife, who has in the meantime become a priestess of Diana, Apollonius thanks the goddess that "you restored me to life."[89]

Iamblichus, in his *Babylonian Story*, features not only an empty tomb story, as we saw above, but yet another apparent death as well. The maid Sinonis is missing. Her father discovers a half-de-voured female corpse and jumps to the conclusion that it is that of his lost daughter. He hangs himself on the spot, but not before inscribing in blood, "Lovely Sinonis lies buried here." Arriving on the scene not long afterward, Sinonis' lover Rhodanes despairs and is about to stab himself, but another woman appears and shouts, "It is not Sinonis lying there, Rhodanes."

A friend of the two lovers, Soraechus, "is condemned to be crucified," but while "being led away to be crucified," Soraechus is rescued by a band of soldiers who drive away his guards.

> But in the meantime, Rhodanes, too, was being led to and hoist-ed onto the cross that had been designated for him by a dancing and garlanded Garmus, who was drunk and dancing round the cross with the flute players and reveling with abandon. While this is happening, Sacas informs Garmus by letter that Sinonis is marrying the youthful king of Syria. Rhodanes rejoices high up on the cross, but Garmus makes to kill himself. He checks himself, however, and brings down Rhodanes from the cross against his will (for he prefers to die [seeing that his beloved is to marry another].)"[90]

Apuleius's *The Golden Ass* contains two scenes which bear an uncanny resemblance to the gospels' scenes at the empty tomb of Jesus, though neither is exactly analogous to them. Employing

---

88. Sandy, in Reardon, *Greek Novels*, p. 769.
89. Sandy, in Reardon, *Greek Novels*, p. 770.
90. Sandy, in Reardon, *Greek Novels*, p. 793.

forbidden necromancy, some seek to question the ghost of a murdered man in order to discover the identity of his slayer.

> "Behold here is one Zatchlas, an Egyptian, who is the most principal prophesier in all this country, and who was hired of me long since to bring back the soul of this man from hell for a short season, and to revive his body from the threshold of death for the trial hereof", and therewithal he brought forth a certain young man clothed in linen raiment . . .[91]

We are readily put in mind of the young man in white at the empty tomb in Mark's gospel.

Second, in the romance of *Cupid and Psyche* we find a scene in which Psyche's sisters seek her out, fearing her dead.

> After a long search made, the sisters of Psyche came unto the hill where she had been set on the rock, and cried with a loud voice and beat their breasts, in such sort that the rocks and stones answered again their frequent howlings: and when they called their sister by her name, so that their lamentable cries came down the mountain unto her ears, she came forth, very anxious and now almost out of her mind, and said: "Behold, here is she for whom you weep; I pray you torment yourself no more, and dry those tears with which you have so long wetted your cheeks, for now may you embrace her for whom you mourned."[92]

A typical sham death and resurrection due to poisoning meets us later in the novel. An evil step-mother has secured from a physician a vial of poison with which to dispatch her step-son who, like Joseph in Genesis, has rebuffed her illicit advances. But the doctor can't help suspecting some chicanery, and he sells her only a potent knock-out formula. So in the midst of the inquest, he leads the mourners to the coffin where a surprise awaits them (though

---

91. Lucius Apuleius, *The Golden* Ass. Trans. William Adlington, rev. Harry C. Schnur (New York: Collier Books, 1962), p. 62.

92. Apuleius, p. 118.

by now we know what to expect).

> every man had a desire to go to the sepulchre where the child
> was laid: there was none of the justices, none of any reputation
> of the town, nor any indeed of the common people, but went
> to see this strange sight. Amongst them all the father of the
> child removed with his own hands the cover of the coffin, and
> found his son rising up after his dead and soporiferous sleep:
> and when he beheld him as one risen from the dead he em-
> braced him in his arms; and he could speak never a word for his
> present gladness, but presented him before the people [cf. Luke
> 7:15] with great joy and consolation, and as he was wrapped and
> bound in the clothes of the grave [cf. John 11:44], so he brought
> him before the judges.[93]

The step-mother is exiled, her henchman "hanged on a gal-
lows," or literally, crucified. Once again we have the immediate
association of crucifixion with an empty tomb.

Petronius' *Satyricon* repeats a well-known tale which juxta-
poses the same two features again. A woman of Ephesus is so
devoted to her late husband that she decides to enter the tomb
with him, there to starve herself to death, joining him in the great
Hereafter. A servant keeps vigil with her. Meanwhile a company
of thieves are crucified nearby.

> Next night the soldier who was guarding the crosses to prevent
> anyone removing one of the corpses for burial noticed a light
> shining among the tombs and, hearing the sound of someone
> mourning, he was eager to know . . . who it was and what was
> going on. Naturally he went down into the vault and seeing a
> beautiful woman, at first stood rooted to the spot as though
> terrified by some strange sight.[94]

---

93. Apuleius, p. 241.

94. Petronius, *The Satyricon*, and Seneca, *The Apocolcyntosis*. Trans.
J.P. Sullivan (Baltimore: Penguin Books, 1977), p. 120.

The soldier brings some food and urges her to eat. He tries to comfort her in her loss. The servant accepts the food and begins to echo the kindly soldier's urgings. "What good is it ... for you to drop dead of starvation, or bury yourself alive ... ? ... Won't you come back to life?" This advice proves persuasive. Not only does the widow break her fast; she is so infused with the *joi de vivre* that she fornicates with the soldier right there in the tomb. "The doors of the vault were of course closed, so if a friend or a stranger came to the tomb, he thought that the blameless widow had expired over her husband's body."[95]

With all this going on, the family of one of the crucified thieves, noticing that the crosses are unattended, "took down the hanging body in the dark and gave it the final rites." The frisky soldier, exiting the tomb, finds one cross empty and knows what must lie in store for him for leaving his post. He is about to kill himself when his new lover suggests he "take the body of her husband from the coffin and fix it to the empty cross." Not a bad idea![96]

Here a dead man exits his tomb only to be crucified and thus save the life of the soldier and bring a new lease on life to his now no longer grieving widow! It almost looks as if the elements of the story of the crucified and resurrected savior in the gospels are reshuffled but are all present. There is even the element of a crucified dead man disappearing despite the posting of guards, somewhat recalling Matthew's empty tomb account!

Another Matthean peculiarity is paralleled in Book IV of Philostratus' *Life of Apollonius of Tyana*. In chapter XVI the sage makes a pilgrimage to the tomb of Achilles. He calls out, like Jesus to Lazarus,

> O Achilles, ... most of mankind declare you are dead, but I cannot agree with them ... show ... yourself to my eyes, if you should be able to use them to attest your existence." Thereupon a slight earthquake shook the neighborhood of the barrow [cf.

---

95. Petronius, p. 121.
96. Petronius, pp. 120–122.

Matt. 28:1–2], and a youth issued forth five cubits high, wearing a cloak of Thessalian fashion ... but he grew bigger, till he was twice as large and even more than that; at any rate he appeared .. to be twelve cubits high just at that moment when he reached his complete stature, and his beauty grew apace with his length.[97]

The Suffering Wise Man

As Charles H. Talbert[98] has shown, the canonical gospels, even in their present form, would not have been hard for an ancient reader to recognize as official hero biographies compiled by a philosophical movement to glorify their founder. It seems to me that Mack, Koester and Robinson would all shy away from such a conclusion, given the prominence of the Passion Story in the canonical gospels. The notion of an atoning death does not seem to fit the picture of the philosophical aretalogy. But it is hardly clear, at least in Mark and Luke, that the idea of an atonement has much to do with it.[99] It may be Helmut Koester's and Theodore J. Weeden's Lutheran background that tempts them to read a theology of the cross into Mark, when only two brief texts could even possibly be read that way (Mark 10:45 and 14:24), and Luke chops even these (Luke 22:27 and 22:18).

As George W.E. Nickelsburg[100] notes (in company with Burton Mack, John Dominic Crossan and others), the story of Jesus' arrest, humiliation, and crucifixion seems to be derived from a

---

97. Philostratus, *The Life of Apollonius* of Tyana, Loeb Classical Library. Trans. F.C. Conybeare (Cambridge: Harvard University Press, 1912) Vol. I, pp. 377, 379. Cf. the gigantic risen Jesus in the Gospel of Peter.

98. Charles H. Talbert, *What is a Gospel? The Genre of the Canonical Gospels* (Philadelphia: Fortress Press, 1977); cf. Dennis R. MacDonald, *Mythologizing Jesus: From Jewish Teacher to Epic Hero* (New York: Rowman & Littlefield, 2015).

99. Robert M. Price, "The Marginality of the Cross." *Journal for Unification Studies*. Vol. VI, 2004–2005, pp. 23–38.

100. George W.E. Nickelsburg, "The Genre and Function of the Markan Passion Narrative." *Harvard Theological Review* 73, pp. 153–184.

whole different cluster of ideas from that of an atonement theology. Rather, the story is probably intended as a typical story of
the wise man who endures all the depredations of the wicked, to
whose sin he is a living rebuke. Such a righteous one is always
either saved in the nick of time or glorified after death. It is easy
to see Jesus' crucifixion account in these terms. And this is the sort
of thing we would expect to find in a community like the Q par-
tisans, as Mack understands them. The Q community could easily
have produced such a hero biography, such a novelistic aretalogy,
issuing in the persecution and deliverance of their hero, the wise
man/sophist Jesus.

But didn't the story of the persecuted wise one usually end
with the rescue of the hero? Yes, though Mack and Crossan apparently feel that a posthumous reward would not violate the logic of
the story. It would be a natural variation on the theme. But would
it? The notion of the wise man having the last laugh at the expense
of his enemies, like Joseph or Daniel, boils down to the funda-
mental idea that "wisdom is the best policy," that "nice guys finish
first." Wisdom is implicitly enlightened self-interest, the Socratic
dictum that if people knew better, they would always do the vir-
tuous thing—because they would see that it is always in their own
best interests! Not, "Do the right, and let the chips fall where they
may," but rather, "Here's how to succeed." The Book of Proverbs
wasn't asking anybody to be a martyr. No, the idea was, you would
ultimately escape the fowler's snare of the wicked.

But maybe the aretalogy of Jesus did fit the pattern anyway.
Remember, the literary devices of the ancient novel included people surviving crucifixions and getting entombed alive. What if an
earlier version pursued the logic of the tale of the wise sufferer to
the letter—and had Jesus survive crucifixion, appearing *still* alive,
not alive *again*? Even in the canonical gospels there are striking
hints of a barely-erased pre-canonical version that read precisely
this way. Muslim interpreters of the gospels have seen some of
these hints, but it is only with the advent of modern narrative
criticism that the clues have become visible to any of the rest of us.

For instance, why does Mark show Jesus asking his Father to allow him to escape death on the cross in Gethsemane? This is exceedingly odd, even offensive, to write unless you are planting a seed that will blossom later in the story. Likewise, for Mark to have Jesus repeating Psalm 22, a prayer anticipating final deliverance even at the last moment, creates all manner of problems unless this prayer, too, is to be answered by story's end. Did Jesus think his God had forsaken him? No, of course not. As the Letter to the Hebrews says, his loud cries and tears were heard, his prayer for deliverance from death answered (Heb. 5:7). Otherwise, again, what was the point of the strange detail of Pilate marveling that Jesus was dead after a mere six hours, when it ought to take days for the cross to kill? As Chekov said, if a writer says somebody drove a nail into the wall, he'd better make sure to hang something from it later in the story! And, obviously, the pay-off would have been that Jesus had fallen into a coma, which ironically, providentially, resulted in his being removed from the cross in time for him to survive.

And why does Matthew have Joseph of Arimathea bury Jesus in Joseph's own tomb (Matt. 27:57–60)? And why does Matthew add the note that Joseph was rich (27:57)? Why, simply to provide narrative motivation for tomb robbers to come and open the tomb, as in the ancient romances, and find Jesus alive! The fainting of Matthew's guards (27:4) probably reflects the terror of the superstitious tomb robbers, finding a living man but no treasure. And then, in Luke 24:36–43, when Jesus appears to his bereaved disciples who assume he is dead and cannot believe their eyes, what does he say to reassure them? Like Apollonius of Tyana says in a similar scene, after a miraculous escape from the treacherous designs of Domitian, he bids his friends to behold his living physical body, to convince themselves that he has not risen from the realm of the dead. He is no ghost, but rather, as his solid corporeality attests, he is *still* alive.

John knew that some people understood the story this way, which is why he adds two items unprecedented in any other gospel: the nailing of Jesus to the cross (often people were simply tied to the cross) in John 20:25 and the spear-thrust in John 19:34. He protests too much (John 19:35), in the style of the writers of apocrypha (cf. 2 Pet. 1:16–18), that he was there and saw the blood flood. In his version, Jesus shows, not his *solid* hands and feet (as in Luke 24:39), but rather his *wounded* hands and *side* (John 20:20). John doesn't want anyone thinking Jesus survived the cross and went to preach among the Greeks (John 7:35).

In this chapter I have tried to show that very much of the Jesus story seems to be structured along the lines of three related contemporary literary genres: the aretalogy of the divine man (*theios aner*), the romantic adventure novel, and the story of the suffering wise man. Various elements that are not characteristic of these three genres can readily be ascribed to interpolations by canonical evangelists/redactors from still other religious sources, specifically rival and/or fossil forms of Jesus sectarianism (of which we shall see still more). But in this chapter it has become especially clear that the gospel epic is a work of literature, not of history. Bracket the literary material and what is left?

5

EPIPHANIES OF YAHWEH

It appears to be all the rage these days among conservative New Testament scholars (AKA orthodox apologists) to defend Trinitarianism by means of something of a Christological sleight of hand trick. As far as I can determine, the trend began with Richard Bauckham's essay "God Crucified"[101] and has been welcomed by numerous others with a theological sigh of relief. The approach is based on a feature of Christological debate from several decades ago: Did the New Testament Christians think of Jesus' divinity as *ontological* or only *functional?* The former represented the traditional notion of Jesus possessing a static nature identical to God's (whether the punch line were to turn out to be Tritheism or Trinitarianism, a consequent question). The latter option, functional Christology, was an attempt to head Trinitarian difficulties off at the pass by eschewing confusing (and potentially dangerous) metaphysics. Not so much *who* Jesus *was* as *what* he *did.* We were told this redefinition was more consistent with the supposed character of Semitic thought, allegedly too primitive to venture into Hellenistic territory. This was no insult, mind you, as the hillbilly Hebrews were to be esteemed as "noble savages," innocent of the vagaries of Cloud-Cuckoo Land. Pragmatic, not speculative, don-

---

101. Richard Bauckham, *Jesus and the God of Israel:* God Crucified *and Other Studies on the New Testament's Christology of Divine Identity* (Grand Rapids: Eerdmans, 2009).

tcha know. Back to gospel simplicity!

But this approach was "essentially" a dodge. Oscar Cull-mann[102] and others might have pretended to be transcending a false dichotomy, but really they were just switching sides. It seems to me that Bauckham and company are doing the same two-step. They, too, try to substitute something else for essentialism, this time "identity" and "relations." Jesus shares moral traits with God as described in the Old Testament (though these apologists seem to have "de-warted" Jehovah rather as the Elohist cleaned up the rough-and-tumble depictions of the Patriarchs by the Yahwist.[103] It is no surprise to detect a whiff of homiletical sanctimony in these deliberations.) Jesus is intimately in tune with God and acts in God's place. And this is sufficient to justify our saying that Jesus' identity is "included in the identity of God," and thus Jesus *is* God. But not *a* God, *the* God.[104]

---

102. Oscar Cullmann, *The Christology of the New Testament*. Trans. S. Guthrie and C. Hall (Philadelphia: Westminster Press, 1959).

103. "What kind of deity is it that would be capable of creating angels and men to sing his praises day and night to all eternity? It is, of course, the figure of an Oriental despot, with his inane and barbaric vanity." White-head in Lucien Price, *Dialogues of Alfred North Whitehead*. An Atlantic Monthly Press Book (Boston: Little, Brown and Company, 1954), p. 277. For the Elohist versus the Yahwist see Hermann Gunkel, *Genesis*. Trans. Mark E. Biddle. Mercer Library of Biblical Studies (Macon: Mercer University Press, 1997), pp. lxii–lxiii.

104. The whole enterprise reminds me of the once-epidemic enthusiasm for Process Theology, derived from the work of Alfred North Whitehead. As applied to Christology, e.g., by John B. Cobb (*Christ in a Pluralistic Age* (Philadelphia: Westminster Press, 1975), p. 74) and David Griffin (*A Process Christology* (Philadelphia: Westminster Press, 1973), pp. 217–218), the idea was that, since every moment "incarnates" the previous moments by way of influence, Christians can now happily cast off Nicene essentialism like a filthy garment in favor of a new schema of Jesus as "incarnating" God in the dubious sense that God was the chief determinant of Jesus' character and mission. This strikes me as merely warmed-over Schleiermacher, who reasoned that Jesus, alone of all men, was perfectly "God-conscious" and that this constituted "a veritable existence of God in him" (cf., Friedrich Daniel Ernst Schleiermacher, *The Life of Jesus*. Trans. S. Maclean Gilmour. Lives of Jesus Series (Phila-

The dominance of the distinction between 'functional' and 'ontic' Christology has made it seem unproblematic to say that, for early Christology, Jesus exercises the 'functions' of divine lordship without being regarded as 'ontically' divine. In fact, such a distinction is highly problematic from the point of view of early Jewish monotheism. For this understanding of the unique divine identity, the universal sovereignty of God was not a mere 'function' which God could delegate to someone else. It was one of the key identifying characteristics of the unique divine identity, which distinguished the one God from all other reality. The unique divine sovereignty is a matter of *who God is*. Jesus' participation in the unique divine sovereignty is, therefore, also not just a matter of what Jesus does, but of *who Jesus is* in relation to God. Though not primarily a matter of divine nature or being, it emphatically is a matter of divine identity. It includes Jesus in the identity of the one God.[105]

Obviously, yes *obviously*, this is a gross cop out. It is just a dodge. Bauckham is just reframing the dilemma and by no means resolving it. He insists that first-century Jewish monotheism was expansive and flexible enough to accommodate the kind of notion

---

delphia: Fortress Press, 1975), pp. 103–104), an equivocation derided by D.F. Strauss: "but the very fact that he calls it a real existence shows that he rather senses that it is an unreal one" (David Friedrich Strauss, *The Christ of Faith and the Jesus of History: A Critique of Schleiermacher's The Life of Jesus*. Trans. Leander E. Keck. Lives of Jesus Series (Philadelphia: Fortress Press, 1977), pp. 24–25.).

105. Bauckham, *Jesus and the God of Israel*, pp. 30–31.You'll find the same approach in, e.g., H. Douglas Buckwalter, *The Character and Purpose of Luke's Christology*. Society for New Testament Studies Monograph Series 89 (New York: Cambridge University Press, 1996): "Luke portrays the exalted Jesus as God's co-equal by the kinds of things he does from heaven. Through the Holy Spirit, the divine name, and personal manifestations, Jesus behaves toward people in Luke-Acts as does Yahweh in the Old Testament. His power and knowledge are supreme. As the Father's co-equal, Jesus sovereignly reigns over Israel, the church, the powers of darkness, and the world." N.p. abstract; Robert F. O'Toole, *Luke's Presentation of Jesus: A Christology*. Subsidia Biblica 25 (Rome: Editrice Pontifico Istituto Biblico, 2004), Chapter Nine, "Luke Predicates the Same or Similar Things of Jesus and of God," pp. 207–224.

he proposes. And what does that mean? Crickets. I think of the theological throat-clearing of the Hanbalite Muslim apologists who insisted that, though Allah hath real bodily members, he remaineth completely non-anthropomorphic. All we can say is that *both* are true, but "without how."[106] Here's the logic as I see it: the New Testament says the same things about both God and Jesus, which might seem to imply they are twin deities, but that cannot be since there is only one Jewish God. The irresistible force meets the immovable object. How does this work itself out? I guess we'll have to wait for that Theology class, taught by angels, in the Hereafter. How is this any better, any more manageable, than the Trinity? How is it *not* the Trinity?

Joachim Jeremias noted that Jesus was modeling God's concern for the lost, as described in his parables of the Prodigal Son and the Lost Sheep, when he sought out the publicans and sinners.[107] Of course. But would this entitle us to "include Jesus' identity in God's"? That is a wild leap if you ask me. (And Jeremias did not make it.) In this connection I think of two quotations. John F. Kennedy said, "Here on earth, God's work must truly be our own." Are we then to be included in the divine identity? And this from Woody Allen's character Ike in the movie *Manhattan*. His friend Yale, rebuked by Ike for a moral betrayal, retorts: "You are so self-righteous, you know? I mean, we're just *p*eople, we're just human beings, you know? You think you're *God!*" Ike replies, "I—I *got*ta model myself after *some*one!"[108]

It's not that Bauckham and company are wrong to point out the Yahweh/Jesus similarities in both character and divine functions. They just don't know what to do with them. Maybe it's time

---

106. Ignaz Goldziher, *Introduction to Islamic Theology and Law*. Trans. Andras and Ruth Hamori. Modern Classics in Near Eastern Studies (Princeton: Princeton University Press, 1981), p. 92.

107. Jeremias, *Parables of Jesus*, p. 132.

108. Woody Allen and Marshall Brickman, "Manhattan." In *Four Films of Woody Allen: Annie Hall, Interiors, Manhattan, Stardust Memories* (New York: Random House, 1982), p. 265.

to go back to the drawing board. In fact, Margaret Barker[109] already has. She and other historians of ancient Israelite religion have, as it were, excavated from the Old Texts themselves (plus other, Canaanite, texts) a coherent and compelling outline of what we might call the pre-Judaic Hebrew religion, a religion of monarchial polytheism exactly parallel to the religion of El and Baal. The chief Hebrew God was El Elyon, God Most High, the Ancient of Days. Menaced by Chaos Dragons called Leviathan/Nehushtan, Behemoth, and Rahab, the Hebrew gods appealed to Elyon's Son, Yahweh, a mighty warrior riding a cloud chariot through the sky and wielding potent thunderbolts. He managed to vanquish these denizens of the Deep (the *Tehom*) and was rewarded with elevation to co-regency alongside his Father (Dan. 7:13–14). Just change some of the names and you've got the mythology of Canaan and Babylon, Israel's ancient neighbors.

This all fell from favor as of the Deuteronomic Reform movement. Yahweh and Elyon were merged into a single deity with two names/epithets. The lesser Sons of God were demoted to the status of mere angels. The Satan (hitherto God's security chief and prosecutor) morphed into Satanael, the sinister enemy of God. The Messiah, formerly a divine king, received a new and more modest job description as a mortal king who should restore the Davidic dynasty. Much had changed, but not everyone went along with it, no more than all Roman Catholics fell in line with the innovations of Vatican II or all Black Muslims acquiesced to the sweeping changes decreed by Wareeth Deen Muhammad after the death of his father, the Honorable Elijah Muhammad. We can be sure that very many Jews simply ignored the "modernism" of the Deuteronomists. They reasoned that what was true last night did not become false this morning by the fiat of some self-appointed religious elite.

Barker showed how Israelite polytheism, ditheism, angelology, and mythology survived underground with a superficial Deuter-

---

109. Margaret Barker, *The Great Angel: A Study of Israel's Second God* (Louisville: Westminster/John Knox Press, 1992).

onomic veneer, much as the Vodun deities (*loa*) continued under the names of the Catholic saints. But not everyone even bothered with such camouflage, and that old-time religion kept going without missing a beat. This is evident in the New Testament if you know what you're looking at. For instance, seven-headed Leviathan is alive and sporting in the Book of Revelation. And Satan! The "official" view of Satan, the Ahriman-like god of Evil, somehow retains his old job, not so much *tempting* as *testing* Jesus (Mark 1:12–13; Matt. 4:1–11; Luke 4:1–13), his apostles (Luke 22:31), and persecuted Christians generally (Rev. 12:10).

We are dealing with grass-roots pre-Deuteronomic belief when we read that the demon addressed Jesus as "Son of the Most High God" (Mark 5:7); i.e., El Elyon. As in Deuteronomy 32:7–9, Yahweh is the Son, one of the Sons, of El Elyon, the one in charge of Israel. Barker reasons that even the shorter title of Jesus, "Son of God," denotes "Son of El (Elyon)." Jesus is never said to be "the Son of the Lord," i.e., "the Son of Yahweh." And there is one obvious reason for that: Jesus *is* Yahweh.[110] He is a theophany like those we find in the Old Testament (Gen. 16:7–13; Exod. 3:1–6; Judg. 6:11–23; chapter 13) when flabbergasted mortals encounter "the Angel of Yahweh," who turns out to *be* Yahweh himself: "Have I really seen Yahweh and lived to tell the tale?"

The problem is that Bauckham and the others take for granted the Deuteronomic soldering together of El and Yahweh but then try to add Jesus into the formula as "included in the identity of Yahweh" yet in some unknown manner not amounting to a second God. What does it all add up to? Not Trinitarianism, I'm afraid, but *polytheism*, or, if you prefer, binitarianism, "two powers in heaven."[111]

---

110. Barker, *Great Angel*, pp. 4–5.

111. Alan F. Segal, *Two Powers in Heaven: Early Rabbinic Reports about Christianity and Gnosticism.* Library of Early Christology (Waco: Baylor University Press, 2012); Peter Schäfer, *Two Gods in Heaven: Jewish Concepts of God in Antiquity* (Princeton: Princeton University Press, 2020).

He Cometh and he Passeth by

G.A. Wells,[112] for many years the chief exponent of the Christ Myth theory, hypothesized that the "appearances" listed in 1 Corinthians 15:3–8 need not and should not be read as postscripts to life-of-Jesus narratives such as we find in the present gospels. Instead, Wells suggested, they were as likely to have denoted apparitions of some figure from the past, even the distant past, like the numerous tales of the prophet Elijah sporadically popping up here and there to rescue the pious. On this understanding, the gospel "histories" of a human Jesus teaching, performing miracles, and submitting to crucifixion were subsequent attempts to historicize the Jesus epiphanies, to provide a back story. The gospel Jesus, then, was "reverse-engineered" from a small set of discrete visitations from on high. And those original visitations were not analogous to ghost sightings, like that of Jacob Marley, but rather to the Old Testament Yahweh theophanies. And not merely analogs to such "close encounters" but simply more of the same. Jesus was Yahweh, or if you like, the Angel of Yahweh. Once he had appeared to Hagar, to Moses, to Gideon. Now he appeared to Cephas, Paul, and Mary Magdalene.

One might venture to say that such was the logical implication of the work of the very boldest form-critics like Bultmann, for whom virtually all of the sayings and deeds ascribed to the pre-Easter Jesus were in fact inventions of the "post-Easter" Christians, the "creative community," materials fabricated (like the hadith of Muhammad) in order to provide guidance for the faithful and to authenticate such guidance as coming "from the Lord." We now take for granted that the commandments of the Torah, with all their sacrificial recipes, temple\furniture, dietary menus, and curtain designs, were only fictively ascribed to the Voice of God speaking to Moses. What's the difference?

May there not be a broad hint of this in the enigmatic "end-

---

112. G.A. Wells, *Did Jesus Exist?* (London: Elek/Pemberton, 1975), p. 32.

ing" of Mark's gospel? His tomb is found to be unoccupied save for a young man draped in white who reminds the visitors that Jesus had instructed the disciples to meet him in Galilee after his resurrection. As Doughty noted, it is easy to read this as a pointer for the reader to go back to the beginning of Mark's narrative when Jesus accosts Peter and Andrew, then the sons of Zebedee busy at their nets in the Sea of Galilee, inviting them to follow him and henceforth to cast their lines for human souls. Isn't this the same story we read in John chapter 21? Only there the disciples, disillusioned at the death of Jesus, have given up evangelism to return to their former, mundane tasks. And then Jesus appears on the shore and bids them follow him. Is this a resurrection narrative, or an initial recruitment story? Perhaps it is both. Perhaps it is the "Risen" Jesus, he who holds all authority in heaven and on earth, who strides the earth through the whole story. Is it not the voice of Yahweh we hear when Mark 9:19 has Jesus speaking as a god impatient with foolish mortals who are wasting his time? "O faithless generation! How long am I to be with you? How long must I bear with you?"

Assuming the Form of a Man

The episode of Jesus' appearance to Mary Magdalene in John chapter 20 seems to owe a debt to that of the self-disclosure of the angel Raphael at the climax of the Book of Tobit.[113] When Tobias first saw Raphael, he "did not know" he was really an angel (Tobit 5:5), just as, when Mary stood weeping outside the tomb, she first saw Jesus there, she "did not know" who he really was (20:14). Having delivered Tobias' fiancé Sarah from her curse, Raphael reveals himself to Tobit and his son Tobias and announces, "I am ascending to him who sent me" (Tobit 12:20), just as Jesus tells Mary, "I am ascending to my father and your father, to my God and your God" (John 20:17). Why does the risen Jesus warn

---

113. Helms, *Gospel Fictions*, pp. 146–147.

Mary "Touch/hold me not, for I have not yet ascended to the father" (20:17a)? This is probably an indication of *docetism*, that Jesus cannot be touched, not having a fleshly body.[114] The reason for seeing docetism here is the parallel it would complete between John 20 and the Raphael revelation/ascension scene, where the angel explains (Tobit 12:19), "All these days I merely appeared to you and did not eat or drink, but you were seeing a vision" (i.e., a semblance).

Luke 4:29–30 also implies divine/angelic intangibility for Jesus. "And they rose up and put him out of the city, and led him to the brow on which their city was built, that they might throw him down headlong. But passing through the midst of them he went away." Where'd he go? He was here just a minute ago! In all this, remember I am not saying any canonical gospel promotes docetic Christology. Rather, my point is that certain odd bits and pieces that appear to contradict the general trend of these gospels can be extracted and placed in something like their pre-canonical contexts in the hypothesized "gospels behind the gospels." And in this case, a pre-gospel of Jesus as a Yahweh theophany, there survive several intriguing bits.

For instance, these portions of the Apocryphal Acts of John, as the Son of Zebedee reminisces about the good old days of the non-incarnation of his Lord. This document dates from about the same time as the better-known Gospel of John. The Acts of John, particularly the section called The Preaching of John, which may well have originally been an independent document in its own right, is probably the clearest and the most extreme exemplar of docetism, as we will shortly see. It forms something of a contrast to John's gospel as usually understood, as in Udo Schnelle's *Anti-Docetic Christology in the Gospel of John*.[115] There are indeed, scat-

---

114. The story was not originally followed by the Doubting Thomas story with its tactile proofs, hence need not be consistent with it. Note, too, that in 20:17b Jesus seems to anticipate not seeing the disciples again. "Tell them goodbye for me."

115. Udo Schnelle, *Antidocetic Christology in the Gospel of John: An In-*

tered through the Gospel, for instance, anti-docetic jabs like John 1:14, "The Word became flesh and dwelt among us." Also, John 4:7 shows Jesus asking someone to "Give me a drink." Likewise, in 19:28b, spread-eagled on the cross, he gasps out, "I thirst." Back in 6:51–57 he says one must eat his flesh and drink his blood to be saved. When he appears alive to Doubting Thomas in 20:27, he invites him to probe his flesh wounds. It seems clear that the Johannine evangelist was pointedly rebutting a rival, a docetic, Christology.

But then, on the other hand, a second look tells a different tale. John 1:14 actually minimizes the idea of incarnation since the word usually rendered "dwelt" is literally "tabernacled," or "pitched his tent" among us. This implies but a temporary stay, and perhaps even an insubstantial veiling, as in Charles Wesley's great hymn with the line "Veiled in flesh the Godhead see." That doesn't sound like incarnation to me. More like what Ernst Käsemann[116] called "naïve docetism."

Apparently Jesus in chapter 4 is just setting up the Samaritan woman for his discourse about living water, because, when it is done, we see him disdain the food the disciples offer him, explaining that he has no need of material nourishment after all: "I have food to eat of which you know nothing, ... for my food is to do the will of him who sent me and to accomplish his [assigned] work" (John 4:32, 34). Note that this is not the same contrast as in Deuteronomy 8:3: "Man shall not live by bread alone, but by every word that comes from the mouth of God." The Johannine Jesus is saying he does not subsist on bread *at all*, but on the will of God.[117] That's docetism. Similarly, does Jesus actually suffer thirst on the cross? Apparently not, since it turns out he said what he said sim-

---

vestigation of the Place of the Fourth Gospel in the Johannine School. Trans. Linda M. Maloney (Minneapolis: Fortress Press, 1992).

116. Ernst Käsemann, *The Testament of Jesus: A Study of the Gospel of John in Light of Chapter 17.* Trans. Gerhard Krodel (Philadelphia: Fortress Press, 1968), p. 26.

117. Käsemann, *Testament of Jesus*, p, 8.

ply in order to follow the script dictated by prophecy (19:28a).

The Risen Jesus invites Thomas to feel his wounds—*but he doesn't!* And in any case, displaying one's wounds for identification's sake is a well-attested device in ancient ghost stories.[118] In such tales, the point is not the fleshly character of the returned dead, but rather confirmation of their identity: "Yes, that's how they killed him, all right!"

What about the Bread of Life discourse with its metaphorical cannibalism? It is only Jesus' stubborn opponents who take him to be referring to literal flesh and blood (John 6:52). That he is not is amply confirmed in verse 63 when he explains: "It is the spirit that gives life; the flesh counts for nothing. The words I have spoken to you are spirit and life."

Why this back-and-forth? Why these mixed signals? I believe we are reading a scribal conflation of two redactions of the Gospel of John, one inclined to incarnationism, the other to docetism. We read of just such a factional rift in 1 John 4:1–6. I infer that each had its own version of the Gospel of John and that some later scribe found himself with copies of both and, as was the instinct of scribes, dared not leave anything out for fear of omitting any of the sacred text.

But there is certainly no ambiguity or equivocation as to the illusory character of Jesus' "body"[119] in the Acts of John.

> I would try to catch him off guard, and never once did I see his eyes blinking; they were constantly open. And often he would appear to me as short and ugly, and then again as a man tall as the sky. Also, another marvel about him: when I reclined next to him at mealtime and leaned back against him to ask him something, sometimes I felt his breast as smooth and soft, but other times hard as stone. Thus I was inwardly troubled and reflected,

---

118. Robert Conner, *Apparitions of Jesus: The Resurrection as Ghost Story* (Valley: Tellectual Press, 2018), pp. 114–115.

119. When 1 Corinthians 15 describes the resurrected form of the believers as a "spiritual body" as opposed to the "natural body" surely the envisioned spiritual body is a docetic one.

"How can I be experiencing this?" And as I thought about this, he turned and said to me, "John, you see yourself in me: if your own heart is tender, then I am tender to your touch; but if your heart is stony, then thus also will you find me."

And another time he takes me, James, and Peter along with him into the mountain where he was accustomed to pray, and we saw shining forth from within him a light no mortal words can begin to describe. A second time he brought us three up into the mountain, and he said, "Come with me." And we went again. And we watched him pray at some distance. So I, being his favorite, approached him quietly, supposing he could not hear me. I stood gazing at his back, [Exod. 33:17–23] and I could see that he was completely undressed; rather, we saw him naked, and not at all like any mere mortal, for his feet were whiter than mountain snow, so that the surrounding ground was lit up by his feet. And as for his head, it reached the very sky! I was afraid and cried out. He turned around, now appearing as a man of short stature. He caught hold of my beard, yanked it, and said to me, "John, be no longer without faith, but a believer!" And I said, "But what have I done wrong, Lord?" And I tell you, brothers, I felt such pain for thirty days where he had yanked my beard that I remarked to him, "Lord, if your mere tug made in sport has hurt me so much, what if you had actually struck me?" And he said to me, "Let it be your lesson from now on not to tempt one who cannot be tempted!"

But Peter and James were angry because I spoke with the Lord, and they motioned to me to rejoin them and leave the Lord alone. So I went, and both of them asked me, "The old man who was speaking with the Lord on the summit—who was he? We heard both of them speaking." And I, recalling his great condescension, and his unity behind many faces, as well as his omniscient vigilance over us, replied, "If you want to know that, you will have to ask him."

Again, one time when all of us, his disciples, were lodging in one house in Gennesaret, I alone spied from beneath my blanket to see what he would do. First I heard him say, "John, go to sleep!" So I pretended to sleep, and I saw another like him, and I heard him say to my Lord, "Jesus, those whom you have chosen do not yet believe in you!" And my Lord said to him, "You speak truly; for they are but mortal men."

I will recount another glory, brothers. Sometimes when I would take hold of him, I encountered a solid, material body, while other times when I touched him, the substance was immaterial, as if it did not even exist. And on any occasion he was invited by one of the Pharisees and attended the dinner, we went with him, and our hosts set a roll before each one of us, and he received one as well, and he would bless his own and divide it between us, and everyone was satisfied with so small a morsel, and our own rolls were left over untouched, which amazed our hosts.

And often, as I walked beside him, I wanted to see the impression of his foot, whether his foot left any print on the ground, for it appeared to me that he walked just above the ground, and I never saw a footprint. And I tell you these things, brothers, to encourage your faith in him; but at present it is not permitted for us to speak of his powerful deeds and wonders, for these surpass mortal speech and, perhaps literally, cannot be put into words or heard with the ear.

Did Jesus Claim to be God?

In Exodus 3:14–15 Yahweh reveals his great Name to his chosen representative Moses: "I Am who I Am! Say this to the people of Israel, 'I Am has sent me to you'. . . Say this to the people of Israel, 'Yahweh, the God of your fathers . . . has sent me to you.'" He is explaining the (supposed) derivation of the name Yahweh from the verb *hayah*, "to be." The Gospel of John is often said to depict Jesus as assuming the divine Name "I Am" in his various revelatory self-declarations, "I am the bread of life" (6:35), "I am the light of the world" (8:12), "I am the good shepherd" (10:14), "I am the door" (10:7), "I am the way, the truth, and the life" (14:6), "I am the resurrection" (11:25), etc., But this is not clearly the case.[120] I

---

120. I would grant, however, that John 8:24 ("You will die in your sins unless you believe that I am [he]") and 8:28 ("you will know that I am [he],") may more clearly point in the theophanic direction. But, as for John 8:58 ("Before Abraham was, I am"), I am not so certain, since Jason BeDuhn has demonstrated that it really has to be translated as "I have been since before Abraham came to be," which, nonetheless, is still obviously a claim

prefer the interpretation of the "I am" (ego eimi) as analogous to the self-declarations of the goddess in the Isis Aretalogy,[121] e.g., "I am Isis, the mistress of every land . . . I gave and ordained laws unto men, which no one is able to change." But if those who trace it to the Exodus scene are correct, it would certainly buttress the case I am making that such texts belonged originally to a gospel of Jesus as a Yahweh Theodicy pure and simple.

---

to pre-existence. See Jason David BeDuhn, *Truth in Translation: Accuracy and Bias in English Translations of the New Testament* (New York: University Press of America, 2003), pp. 106–108.

121. Philip B. Harner, *The "I Am" of the Fourth Gospel: A Study in Johannine Usage and Thought.* Facet Books Biblical Series 26 (Philadelphia: Fortress Press, 1970), p. 26.

6

GNOSTIC REVEALER AND REDEEMER

Earlier in this book I ridiculed the tendency of some scholars (apparently being ecumenically sensitive to the feelings of sectarians dead for many centuries) to deny there was ever such a thing as "Gnosticism." If they mean no more than that not all Gnostics agreed at every point, well, that's old news. There is in fact an Ideal Type of Gnosticism. I want to outline some salient features of it here, preparatory to outlining a hypothetical pre-gospel that would have been Gnostic in character.

Gnosticism was anciently dubbed "the hydra-headed heresy"[122] since there were so many versions of it, with greater or lesser differences between them. But it had as many roots as it had fruits. Scholars had hypothesized a number of possible inspirations for Gnosticism including Platonism, Zoroastrianism, Hermeticism, and anti-apocalyptic Hellenistic Judaism. The 1945 discovery of the Nag Hammadi codices seems to have vindicated all of them! The collection included texts from all these traditions, some of them featuring an additional Gnostic veneer. But one can trace the most important feature, that of the Redeemed Redeemer, way back into pre-Jewish Mesopotamian myth.[123]

---

122. "Cut off one head, and two more will take its place!"

123. Geo Widengren, *Mesopotamian Elements in Manichaeism*. King and Saviour II. Studies in Maitet Arsskrift 1946: 3 (Uppsala: A.B. Lundequistska Bokhandeln, 1946).

Gnosticism (like its Indian cousins Jnana Yoga and Jainism and its sixteenth-century counterpart Lurianic Kabbalah) was essentially a form of *theodicy*, a term coined by the philosopher-theologian Leibniz to denote attempts to "justify God," to absolve him from responsibility for the evil in the world. Why is there evil in a world created by a righteous God? The Gnostic answer was that God *didn't* create the world! Someone else did. And he did a pretty slipshod job of it. Gnostics envisioned an ultimate Father at the center of the divine Pleroma ("fullness"), an ocean of spiritual light. This Being emanated pairs ("syzygies") of subordinate beings called Aions. Each pair generated the next. Valentinus (supposedly a disciple of Theodas, a disciple of Paul) taught that there finally turned out to be no less than 365 Aions. But that's an odd number, right? The last pair of Aions generated only a single being, Lady Wisdom. She straddled the rim of the Pleroma, so far from the center that she had no idea what went on there. And she wanted a baby Aion of her own. (I gather this was a double way of saying she wanted to "conceive," i.e., both an offspring and an idea.) What was she to do? Somehow she contrived a virginal conception, giving birth to an inferior being called the Demiurge ("craftsman"). He was called "Ialdabaoth" (Yahweh Sabaoth), the Creator God of the Old Testament.

He initially imagined himself to be the only God ("I am Yahweh; there is no God beside me!"), but his mother quickly set him straight, mocking him as "Saklas" (the Blind One). His creation was composed of inert matter, lifeless and unmoving. Some said Ialdabaoth managed to collect the divine light of his mother's reflection in the muddy lake of his creation, and these sparks he inserted into his mud-pie homunculi, churning out a human race of fleshly Golems.

Others imagined that the Archons (i.e., Archangels), henchmen created by the Demiurge, ambushed and abducted one of the bright Aions, the Man of Light (or Primal Man or Heavenly Adam). They siphoned off enough of his constitutive photons to give life and motion to the Demiurge's puppets. Most humans lacked inner divine sparks, i.e., spirits. Sure, they possessed souls, but (as Yoga and Non-dualism also taught) the soul is itself material in nature (as we would say, electro-chemical). These were called the *psuchikoi* ("soulish ones" or "natural ones"). They included the conventionally religious who had been tricked into worshipping the Archons and the Demiurge, unaware of the higher God. Lower still were the *hylics* ("wooden ones") or *sarkikoi* ("carnal ones"), little more than dumb animals, whether docile grazers or vicious predators. The elites, like flashlights powered by the divine batteries of implanted light, were called *pneumatikoi* ("spiritual ones").

There were not enough divine photons to go around (otherwise perhaps everyone might get one) because the captured Man of Light managed to escape with most of his photons intact, returning to the Pleroma. Eventually he returned, his mission to retrieve or rescue his stolen sparks. He is both Revealer and, by the same token, Redeemer. He appears in human form, seeking out the men and women who possess the spark. They are easily recognized because they are dissatisfied, alienated, feeling themselves strangers in a strange land. The Revealer (like Morpheus in *The Matrix*), is always on the lookout for these individuals, approaching them, empathizing with their discomfort and offering a way out. What they do not suspect but need to know is the truth of their origin and destiny: Their true self is the divine spark, finally at peace in the Pleroma. Once one knows this, one can ascend there upon the death of the material body. As long as one remains ignorant, one will be continuously reincarnated in the Demiurge's vale of tears. The spirit, you see, is immortal, unlike its fleshly container, so the latter must be replaced as each fleshly body wears out. As Socrates said, *soma sema*, the body is the prison house of the soul. And Morpheus is offering you a chance for a prison break. This is why he is also the Redeemer. Part of the knowledge (*gnosis*) he imparts is that of the passwords that will get the ascending spirit past the ever-vigilant Archons who stand posted at each of the concentric spheres surrounding planet earth. In this way the divine photon, the true Self, is liberated, redeemed. Gnostics themselves continued the mission of the initial Redeemer. They were the Gnostic apostles.

The Valentinians, a Christian sect, did not disdain the poor *psuchikoi*. They taught that there was a Plan B for them. They understood Jesus to have been the channeler for the Christ Spirit, identical with the Man of Light. The Christ was the Revealer. His esoteric teaching provided saving knowledge to the *pneumatikoi*, but the man Jesus died on the cross to redeem the pious *psuchikoi*. And the slovenly *sarkikoi*? Well, there was nothing stopping them from repenting and becoming *psuchikoi*. The difference between the pneumatics and both other species was qualitative, that between the psychics and the sarkics simply quantitative.

Today the consensus (i.e., the party line) opinion is that Christianity predates Gnosticism, which grew up as an aberrant mutation thereof.[124] It was not always so. The *Religionsgeschichtliche Schule* (History of Religions School) once held the field, positing just the reverse: Christianity was a composite of various influences, notably Gnosticism, Jewish Apocalypticism, and the Mystery Religions. As I see it, the present consensus is simply part of a theologically motivated rightward turn in New Testament scholarship. It is cut from the same bolt of cloth as the vain attempt to make the dying-and-rising god mytheme a borrowing from Christianity. It is basically apologetics with better footnotes.

> [F]or a long time it was regarded as a purely Christian movement, a perversion of the Christian faith into a speculative theology, 'the acute Hellenization of Christianity'. Further research, however, has made it abundantly clear that it was really a movement of pre-Christian origin, invading the West from the Orient as a competitor of Christianity.[125]

One reason I believe Gnosticism predates Christianity is that,

---

124. E.g., Edwin M. Yamauchi, *Pre-Christian Gnosticism: A Survey of the Proposed Evidences* (Grand Rapids: Eerdmans, 1973).

125. Rudolf Bultmann, *Primitive Christianity in its Contemporary Setting.* Trans. R.H. Fuller (New York: Meridian Books, 1956), p. 162.

as Walter Schmithals[126] suggests, several of the Nag Hammadi Gnostic tracts credit their revelatory content to Seth, Shem,
Adam, or Melchizedek. Why not Jesus, Peter, Paul, and James?
Of course, these latter worthies are given credit for other Gnostic
texts, but why not all? If they're all Christian in origin? Second,
one must ask after the logical direction of influence: from Christianity to Gnosticism? Or from Gnosticism to Christianity? For my
part, Harnack's[127] schema seems more natural: he somewhere says
that early Christianity combined three modules occurring with
integrity in separate movements. The sacraments of initiation look
like those of the ancient Mysteries. The depiction of Jesus as a
miracle-working divine man matches the hero cults. And the notion of Jesus as the visible manifestation of a pre-existent heavenly
being makes sense as a simplification of the Gnostic Redeemer
myth. I recall how, once at the Jesus Seminar, Bruce Chilton made
a striking analogy that applies well here. He told about a weekend
visit to a friend's home. Going into the guest bathroom, he was
amused to note that the several towels each bore the signature
trademark of a different hotel chain: Omni, Marriot, Hilton, etc.
What are the chances that representatives of these hotels had visited this bathroom and that each one borrowed a different logo for
use in his own chain's towels? No, it is of course overwhelmingly
more probable that his host had swiped each one of the towels
from a different hotel he had visited. In the same way, we must ask
whether it is not more natural to infer that Christianity derived
these theological "towels" severally from Gnosticism, Apocalyptic,
and the Divine Man genre than that these three "parted Christianity's garments among them."

The Secret Advent

126. Walter Schmithals, *The Apocalyptic Movement: Introduction and Interpretation*. Trans. John E. Steely (New York: Abingdon Press, 1975), p. 95.

127. Cf., Adolf von Harnack, *Marcion: The Gospel of the Alien God*. Trans. John E. Steely and Lyle D. Bierma (Durham: Labyrinth Press, 1990), p. 4.

The pseudepigraphical apocalypse called the Ascension of Isaiah recounts the clandestine descent of the Savior from the Pleroma:[128]

> And so I saw my Lord go forth from the seventh heaven into the sixth heaven.
>
> And the angel who conducted me [from this world was with me and] said unto me: "Understand, Isaiah, and see the transformation and descent of the Lord."
>
> And I saw, and when the angels saw Him, thereupon those in the sixth heaven praised and lauded Him; for He had not been transformed after the shape of the angels there, and they praised Him and I also praised with them.
>
> And I saw when He descended into the fifth heaven, that in the fifth heaven He made Himself like unto the form of the angels there, and they did not praise Him (nor worship Him); for His form was like unto theirs.
>
> And then He descended into the fourth heaven, and made Himself like unto the form of the angels there.
>
> And when they saw Him, they did not praise or laud Him; for His form was like unto their form.
>
> And again I saw when He descended into the third heaven, and He made Himself like unto the form of the angels in the third heaven.
>
> And those who kept the gate of the (third) heaven demanded the password, and the Lord gave (it) to them in order that He should not be recognized. And when they saw Him, they did not praise or laud Him; for His form was like unto their form.
>
> And again I saw when He descended into the second heaven, and again He gave the password there; those who kept the gate proceeded to demand and the Lord to give.
>
> And I saw when He made Himself like unto the form of the angels in the second heaven, and they saw Him and they did not praise Him; for His form was like unto their form.
>
> And again I saw when He descended into the first heaven, and there also He gave the password to those who kept the gate, and He made Himself like unto the form of the angels who

---

128. http://www.earlychristianwritings.com/text/ascension.html

were on the left of that throne, and they neither praised nor lauded Him; for His form was like unto their form.

But as for me no one asked me on account of the angel who conducted me.

And again He descended into the firmament where dwelleth the ruler of this world, and He gave the password to those on the left, and His form was like theirs, and they did not praise Him there; but they were envying one another and fighting; for here there is a power of evil and envying about trifles.

And I saw when He descended and made Himself like unto the angels of the air, and He was like one of them.

And He gave no password; for one was plundering and doing violence to another.

This colorful vision serves as an elaboration of and a commentary on 1 Corinthians 2:6–8: "Yet among the mature we do impart wisdom, although it is not a wisdom of this age or of the archons of this age, who are doomed to pass away. But we impart a secret and hidden wisdom of God, which God decreed before the ages for our glorification. None of the archons of this age understood this; for if they had, they would not have crucified the Lord of glory." Ascension IX:14–17 ("And the prince of that world will stretch out his hand against the Son, and they will hang him on a tree and will kill him, not knowing who he is.")[129] seems to be a glancing citation of the 1 Corinthians passage, but the description of the Savior assuming the outward form of the angels resident on each successive level of heaven appears to preserve the genuine mythic context assumed by 1 Corinthians rather than a creative midrash based on the verse. At any rate, we must ask, "What is it that the Archons/prince of this world failed to understand?" If they did not recognize Jesus as a dangerous threat, why did they engineer his death? We see the same puzzle when we compare Mark and Matthew with Luke and John. The former two gospels depict Satan as trying to derail Jesus' progress to the cross, as when Peter rebukes

---

129. Trans. R.H. Charles, rev. J.M.T. Barton. In H.F.D. Sparks, ed., *The Apocryphal Old Testament* (Oxford: Clarendon Press, 1984), p. 803.

Jesus for saying he must be crucified and Jesus calls him "Satan" (Mark 8:31–33; Matt. 16:21–23). Peter has unwittingly become a ventriloquist dummy for the devil who doesn't want Jesus hoisted on that cross, though not for the same reason. What is Satan afraid will happen if Jesus follows through on his death?

Luke and John sketch Satan differently. Both have Satan possess Judas Iscariot so he will betray Jesus (Luke 22:3–6; John 13:2). Instead of calling Peter "Satan" as in Mark and Matthew, John has Jesus identify Judas (John 6:70–71) as "the devil." Here Satan *wants* Jesus to die, again for the sake of his own nefarious purposes. What is Satan afraid will happen to him if Jesus *avoids* crucifixion? Apparently Jesus' exaltation ("lifting up") on the cross will dethrone Satan as "the Archon of this world" (John 12:31–32), and Satan does not know this. Luke and John seem to view the Archon of this world as 1 Corinthians 2 viewed the ignorant Archons of this age. They wanted him dead, not knowing their success would mean their own death warrant. Does the Markan/Matthean Satan know what the Lukan/Johannine Satan and the Corinthian Archons do not? In that case, why do the latter want Jesus out of the way? Presumably because Jesus keeps freeing Satan's hostages (Luke 13:16; Acts 10:38). They have no idea what is really at stake. Their plan to eliminate Jesus backfires on them because they did not know to expect the resurrection.

Where the Ascension of Isaiah goes beyond 1 Corinthians is in expanding the secrecy theme to include the process of the Redeemer's journey from the heaven of heavens to this sublunary realm. Jesus did not assume his human form once he appeared in his mother's womb. No, he kept having to switch disguises at each lower level so that none of its residents would recognize him—and detain him! Similarly, he comes prepared with the necessary passwords enabling the Archons to stamp his passport at each planetary checkpoint. What is the point of giving us this "information"? I think it is intended to provide a kind of road map (albeit in reverse direction) for the liberated pneumatic on his journey back home to the Pleroma. For just as the Redeemer was obliged keep straight the names of each Archon to gain passage on the way down, so must the home-going Gnostic on the way up. And just as the Redeemer clothed himself in the concentric bodily layers matching each heavenly sphere, so must the ascending pneumatic strip off each of the seven somatic "bodies" that every human carries about every day here on earth.[130] This part of the story goes untold in the canonical gospels, though, as we have just seen, it retained a place in other early Christian documents. Just as Margaret Barker discerns in various Old Testament Pseudepigrapha fuller versions presupposed in canonical texts (concerning, e.g., the pre-Flood Watchers, the design of the Jerusalem Temple), I venture that the Ascension of Isaiah preserves a fascinating segment of the Jesus story from the gospels behind the gospels.

---

130. Marc Edmund Jones, *Occult Philosophy: An Introduction, the Major Concepts and a Glossary* (Boulder: Shambhala Publications, 1977), p. 329. The seven somatic, internal levels form the microcosm; the seven levels of heaven above constitute the macrocosm. Gnosticism employs the metaphor of rising through the external heavens; Yoga envisions the soul rising through the inner levels to the crown chakra. Both describe the ascent to enlightenment. The seven somatic layers are as follows:

The *Etheric* Body – First Layer

The *Emotional* Body – Second Layer

The *Mental* Body – Third Layer

The *Astral* Body – Fourth Layer

The *Etheric* Template Body – Fifth Layer

The *Celestial* Body – Sixth Layer

The *Causal* Body or Ketheric Template – Seventh Layer

(https://quantumstones.com/fostering-higher-vibrations-seven-subtle-bodies/)

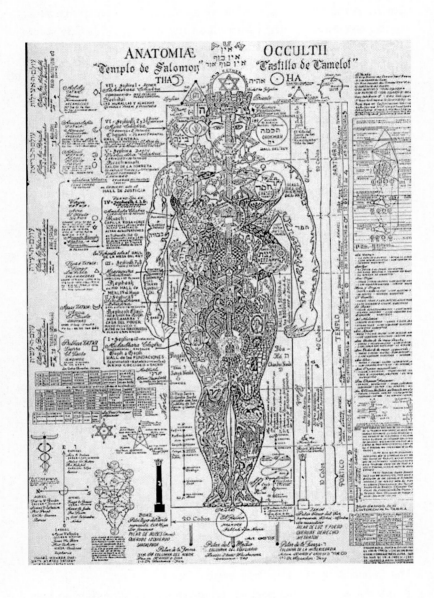

In what mode did the Christ abide while among humans on earth? Some Gnostics were docetists, though you needn't have been a Gnostic to be a docetist. For example, in the main, the second-century Apocryphal Acts were not Gnostic but only ascetic, positing a Jesus too holy to possess a body of solid (sinful) flesh. And, as in the previous chapter, docetism is also a function of angelic theophanies in the Old Testament. Conversely, some Gnostics were not docetists. And among the latter, some were what Bart Ehrman[131] has helpfully dubbed "separationists": they believed that, at the Jordan, the Spirit descended *into* Jesus and thenceforward spoke through him in the manner of our modern channelers. First John 4:1–3 condemns docetism, and 1 John 5:1 blasts separationism. Next I want to set forth some of the anomalous data indicating a pre-canonical separationist Jesus story. First, the baptism.

Steven L. Davies writes, "The story of Jesus' baptism is more than the story of Jesus' repentance and immersion, it is the story of his initial possession experience."[132] Likewise Robert M. Fowler:

> In discussions of Mark's baptism episode . . . the spirit is usually said to descend "upon" Jesus. A more literal rendering of the Greek preposition *eis*, however, would have the spirit descend "into" Jesus. Each of the other evangelists uses *epi*, "upon," describing a more genteel resting of the spirit upon Jesus, and this understanding has usually been read into Mark, but inappropriately, because Mark is portraying for us a person being invaded or possessed by a spirit. In Mark, Jesus becomes spirit-possessed.[133]

---

131. Bart D. Ehrman, *The Orthodox Corruption of Scripture: The Effect of Early Christological Controversies on the Text of the New Testament* (New York: Oxford University Press, 1993), p. 14.

132. Stevan L. Davies, *Spirit Possession and the Origins of Christianity* (Dublin: Bardic Press, 2014), p. 94.

133. Robert M. Fowler, *Let the Reader Understand: Reader-Response Criticism and the Gospel of Mark* (Minneapolis: Augsburg Fortress, 1991), p. 16.

Michael D. Goulder notes that, just as Gnostics were not the only docetists, neither were they the only separationists: "Epiphanius writes interestingly, 'The Ebionites say that the Spirit, which is Christ, came into him and clothed him who was called Jesus' (*Pan.* 30.16.3)."[134] And "the Holy Spirit *descended and entered into* Jesus: such an expression is in line with a possession Christology. Of our Gospels, Mark uses the similar phrase, *descending into him* ... ; but both Matthew and Luke carefully change this to *upon him*."[135] "Mark does not believe the possessionist Christology, but he has left the *into* in by oversight."[136]

This is just what I am envisioning throughout this study: the separationist/possessionist Christology does not really contribute to overall Markan Christology but is instead an incongruent fossil from a previous Jesus story with a different Christology. And we seem perhaps to meet with another such toward the other end of this gospel (Mark 15:34–35).

> The Ebionites thought that Christ left Jesus on the cross: Mark does *not* think that, but he does retain a saying which seems to imply it – according to him Jesus' last words just before he died were, 'My God, my God, why did you forsake me?' ... Just as later Matthew was to re-write Mark to make it more Petrine, so Mark took over the earlier version of the Gospel (whether written or oral). (Goulder)[137]

Is the Christ Spirit forsaking the man Jesus, a la the Gospel of Peter? That fragmentary text has the crucified Jesus cry, "My power, my power, why have you left me?"

A separationist Jesus story might even provide an important clue to the meaning of the enigmatic self-designation of Jesus as the Son of Man. Is it possible that when Jesus speaks of the Son of

---

134. Michael D. Goulder, *St. Paul versus St. Peter: A Tale of Two Missions* (Louisville: Westminster John Knox, 1994), p. 113.

135. Goulder, *St. Paul versus St. Peter*, p. 111.

136. Goulder, *St. Paul versus St. Peter*, p. 130.

137. Goulder, *St. Paul versus St. Peter*, p. 129.

Man, especially of his coming sufferings, it is the Christ Spirit referring to the human Jesus? I prefer this possibility to the attempt of Jack Dean Kingsbury:[138] "'the Son of Man' is a title by means of which Jesus refers to himself in public in order to point to himself as 'the man,' or 'the human being' (this man, or this human being), and to assert his authority in the face of opposition." Is not this a useless tautology, a "definition" by mere denotation? Unless it refers to the human channeler of the Christ.

I think we find in Mark's gospel yet another stray bit of Gnostic, this time Simonian, teaching about the crucifixion. The Pseudo-Clementines inform us that Simon Magus claimed he had previously appeared among the Jews as the Son who seemed to the casual observer to have suffered on the cross but in fact was impervious. If we take a second look at Mark 15:21–24a, we must wonder if the narrative perhaps already presupposes the Simonian teaching.

> And they compelled a passer-by, Simon of Cyrene, who was coming in from the country, the father of Alexander and Rufus, to carry his cross. And they brought him to the place called Golgotha (which means the place of a skull). And they offered him wine mingled with myrrh; but he did not take it. And they crucified him.

Simon Magus hailed from the Samaritan town of Gitta, the old Philistine Gath, also Goliath's home town. "Gitta" thus doubly suggests the Philistines, as the Sea Peoples (including the Philistines) were also called the "Kittim." (Are you still with me?) Mark's "Simon of Cyrene" was thus also "Simon of Gitta," as Cyrene was another old Philistine settlement. Well, so what? The Alexandrian Gnostic Basilides (ostensibly a disciple of Glaukias, in turn a student of Simon Peter) noticed how the pronoun "him" in "they crucified *him*" should rightly refer, not to Jesus, but rather to *Simon of Cyrene* as the last proper name previous to the pronoun! Now

---

138. Kingsbury, *Christology of Mark's Gospel*, p. 83.

if Simon of Cyrene is interchangeable with "Simon of Gitta, i.e., Simon Magus, we have the basis, or the reflection, of the Simonian claim that the Magus had been (painlessly) crucified among the Jews. (Of course I am not arguing that this is actually what happened on Good Friday, but only that this Basilidean-Simonian doctrine may have been another vestige of a Gnostic gospel behind the gospels.

Wise as the Serpent

"And as Moses lifted up the serpent in the wilderness, so must the Son of man be lifted up, that whoever believes in him may have eternal life" (John 3:14–15). This passage is part of a surprisingly long "great chain of meaning." It did not always mean what it means to readers today. Yes, of course the immediate allusion is to Numbers 21:8–9, "And Yahweh said to Moses, 'Make a fiery serpent, and set it on a pole; and every one who is bitten, when he sees it, shall live.' So Moses made a bronze serpent, and set it on a pole; and if a serpent bit any man, he would look at the bronze serpent and live." Yahweh had gotten fed up with the bratty griping of his people in the desert, so he sicced a slithering gang of "fiery," i.e., poisonous, serpents on them in order to thin out the populace a bit. But Moses prevailed upon him to give them a break, prompting God to tell Moses how to construct a magic apotropaic ("turning away") device: it was a bronze model of one of these snakes wound around a pole. If anybody had sustained a bite, he or she need only take a look at this effigy, held aloft, to be healed from the venom. Of course, the bronze serpent is a version of Mercury's caduceus, still the symbol of medicine today. In 2 Kings 18:4 we learn that King Hezekiah "removed the high places, and broke the pillars, and cut down the Asherah. And he broke in pieces the bronze serpent that Moses had made, for until those days the people of Israel had burned incense to it; it was called Nehushtan." At first glance we might think this passage is telling us that the (supposedly original) bronze serpent crafted by Moses centuries before had been placed on display in the Jerusalem Temple, as a relic to memorialize the ancient event. But it immediately becomes clear that more than that is entailed. The thing, after all, had a *name*. And incense was offered to it periodically. Nobody does that with the Liberty Bell. What giveth?

"Nehush*tan*" means "serpent" plus an honorific suffix. It is exactly synonymous with "Levia*than*," one of the Chaos Dragons slain by Yahweh in his bid to gain kingship over the gods and to create the world. It was parallel to the victory of Marduk over Tiamat in the Babylonian creation epic *Enuma Elish*. The Dragons were actually the first generation of gods. Old gods seldom lose all their worshippers even when they are deposed and supplanted, and that is what was happening in the Temple. Yahweh was the main event, but lesser attractions, sideshows, were allowed in the side chapels of the holy precincts. You can also spot vestiges of Nehushtan worship in the theophoric names in the Old Testament (Nahash, King of the Ammonites, and Queen Nehushta). The Edenic Serpent, never called Satan, was instead intended as Nehushtan. He imparted wisdom to Eve and Adam, telling the truth and exploding Yahweh's lies. He was a Prometheus figure. It must have been the work of a Nehushtan priest, unrepentant despite Hezekiah's interdiction of his cult. The worship of the divine Ophidian must have long continued in Israel, as Hippolytus of Rome mentions a pre-Christian[139] Jewish sect of the Naassenes, which must have evolved into the subsequent Gnostic sect of the same name. We are told that they deemed themselves the true Christians and equated Jesus with both Adam and Attis! They claimed their teachings stemmed from James the Just via his disciple Mariamne.

The Naassenes understood John 3:14–15 as equating Jesus with Nehushtan, depicted as the bronze serpent. Those who look

139. L. Gordon Rylands, *The Beginnings of Gnostic Christianity* (London: Watts & Co., 1940), pp. 123–124; Jessie Weston, *From Ritual to Romance* (Cambridge University Press, 1920; rpt. Garden City: Doubleday Anchor Books, 1957), pp. 156–158.

to him, lifted up on his cruciform "pole," will receive the saving *gnosis*. The Fourth Evangelist may or may not have understood it in this way, but it would make a lot of sense as a relic from the "Gnostic Jesus" gospel before the Gospel of John.

The Mystery of the Kingdom of God

Mark's gospel is built around what its most astute reader, William Wrede, called "the Messianic Secret,"[140] which is expressed in Jesus' numerous attempts to keep his healings quiet (though with little success), to silence the demons eager to expose his secret identity, and to hide the fact of his messiahship. But there is another important secret, "the secret of the kingdom of God," not so much revealed as concealed in Jesus' parables. Mark tells us that Jesus preferred this mode of teaching precisely because it would communicate on two levels, to two separate audiences. There was the common run of mankind (what I call the "pew potatoes") on the one hand, and, on the other, those with ears to hear, what Meister Eckhart used to call "the aristocrat[s]."[141] I believe we may apply the same dichotomy to New Testament interpreters. Most seem to take the messages of the parables as a prediction of the eventual triumph of Christianity, or perhaps the imminent dawn of the Apocalypse, or mere gnomic platitudes. For T.A. Burkill, the secret was pretty much just the soon-to-be-preached Christian message of Jesus' atonement and resurrection. But this cannot be right. The Christian plan of salvation, a la Burkill,[142] is a square peg forced into this round hole. The secret of the kingdom of God, which its intended receivers do not seem to grasp, *must* be realized eschatology, a la the Gospel of Thomas, saying 51. "His disciples said to

---

140. William Wrede, *The Messianic Secret*. Trans. J.C.G. Greig (Cambridge: James Clarke, 1971).

141. *Meister Eckhart*. Trans. Raymond Bernard Blakney, Harper Torchbooks (New York: Harper & Row, 1941), pp. 74–81.

142. T.A. Burkill, *Mysterious Revelation: An Examination of the Philosophy of St. Mark's Gospel* (Ithaca: Cornell University Press, 1963).

him: On what day will the repose of the dead come into being? And on what day will the new world come? He said to them: That which ye await has come, but ye know it not." The true meaning could be found at a deeper level by the illuminati who have ears to hear; that is, beneath a surface level of meaning that *does* edify the *psuchikoi*. Mark's parables possess a meaningful albeit superficial sense that satisfies the *psuchikoi*. They weren't left shaking their heads at unintelligible glossolalia. But the *pneumatikoi* will silently nod as they see the deeper meaning. If these parables (some preserved in Mark, some in other gospels) did reveal/conceal Gnostic teaching, pearls to be hidden from the pigs, what might that teaching have been? Who knows? But then it is not too hard to make educated guesses.

The Sower (Mark 4:3–20): The man who scatters the seeds (*logoi spermatikoi*) is the Demiurge, injecting the divine photons into his clay-pigeon creations. But not all even of the potential pneumatics actually come to fruition, since so many are comfortably or uncomfortably numb, though perhaps (as in Buddhism) they will eventually awaken if only in a future incarnation.

The Seed Growing Secretly (Mark 4:26–29) speaks of the alien origin of the divine sparks planted in the soil of this material world. When the unsuspecting possessor of the spark hears the message of transformation, of the emergence of the divine spark from the constricting cocoon of the flesh, he knows it is nothing he could have achieved of himself. But let him not then ignore it and go back to sleep! He must now cultivate the fruit of the Spirit!

The Mustard Seed (Mark 4:30–32): the truth of the gnosis of the kingdom of God surpasses expression, "unutterable utterances that are not lawful for man to utter" (2 Cor. 12:4; cf. the Buddhist Parable of the Tadpole).[143] Nonetheless, once planted in the ear of

---

143. One day a little tadpole asked his dad to tell him what life is like up on dry land. His father, a fine fat frog, regrets he must disappoint the lad. Every word the tadpole knows is completely conditioned by underwater existence. Thus no such words can possibly describe life on the surface. The tadpole will just have to wait.

the hearer, it is sure to bring about a wholesale transformation! It is sown a physical body but raised (in this life) a pneumatic body (1 Cor. 15:35–44).

The Wicked Tenants (Mark 12:1–11): The field is the world. The tenant farmers are the Archons. The landlord is the Father. The anticipated fruits of the harvest are the divine sparks, and the Archons refuse to yield them up. The first emissaries sent to collect them are the "villains" of the Old Testament: the Serpent, Cain, Pharaoh, Korah, Jezebel, Hamaan, etc. The Son is the Gnostic Redeemer, sent to recapture the light stolen from him. His death at their hands harks back to his primordial murder, which necessitates his final mission.

The Wheat and the Tares (Matt. 14:23–30, 36–43): Again, the field is the world. The farmer is the Father. The wheat stalks are those whose germ comes from the Pleroma of the Father, though he was not the one who planted them. The Enemy is the Demiurge. The tares are the fleshly bodies into which the pleromatic sparks are trapped. Do not seek to separate the two prematurely (as the Cathars[144] and Jainists,[145] practitioners of ritual suicide by starvation did), but wait till death separates them.

The Leaven (Matt. 13:33) is parallel to the Mustard Seed, except that it lacks the ineffability element.

The Hidden Treasure (Matt. 13:44) concerns the joy of the liberating knowledge of the unsuspecting spark within.

The Pearl of Great Price (Matt. 13:45–46): What the merchant is willing to trade for the pearl is the formerly valued goods of the material world. It is like Thomas, saying 56, "Jesus said, Whoever has come to understand the world has found but a corpse, and whoever has found a corpse is superior to the world."

The Lost Sheep (Matt. 18:12–14/ Luke 15:3–7): Perhaps Thom-

144. Steven Runciman, *The Medieval Manichee: A Study of the Christian Dualist Heresy* (New York: Viking Press, 1961), pp. 158–159.

145. Walther Schubring, *The Doctrine of the Jainas Described after the Old Sources.* Trans. Wolfgang Beurlen (Delhi: Motilal Banarsidass, 1962), pp. 325–327.

as saying 107 captures the original point: "Jesus said, The kingdom is like a shepherd who had a hundred sheep. One of them, the largest, went astray. He left the ninety-nine sheep and looked for that one until he found it. When he had gone to such trouble, he said to that sheep, 'I care for you more than the ninety-nine.'"This version removes the difficulty that mars the Matthew/Luke parable; the canonical version seems to want to depict the shepherd as equally concerned with every one of the hundred in his charge: he cannot abide the loss of a single one. But then why does he abandon the ninety-nine to their own defenseless devices while he charges off in search of the missing one? But Thomas' shepherd rightly cares naught for the useless, scrawny sweater-candidates. He had been searching the flock for the one he wanted: a nice big one! The Good Shepherd is the Gnostic Redeemer who has nothing to offer the mediocre mass. His business is to ferret out an unsuspecting pneumatic.

The Lost Coin (Luke 15:8–10): It concerns Simon Magus seeking and finding Helen, the long-lost Ennoia, living amid the squalor of the world created by the Archons.

The Prodigal Son (Luke 15:11–32) is an exact parallel to the Hymn of the Pearl embedded in the Acts of Thomas. In that text we read the Gnostic allegory of a Persian prince sent incognito into Egypt on a mission. While there he is distracted by the flashy temptations of exotic Egypt to the point where he actually forgets who he is and why he is there! His father, wondering why his son does not return home with news of his mission, sends him a letter. Reading it jolts the prince back to his proper wits, and, completing his mission, he strips off his Egyptian finery and goes home. Of course, the prince is the Redeemed Redeemer who is submerged in the swampy material world, but he (i.e., his stolen pleromatic photons) is finally restored to enlightened self-knowledge and makes his way back to the Pleroma, where his Father awaits him.

The Good Samaritan (Luke 10:29–37): The point is to show the superiority of (Samaritan) Simonianism over Judaism. The wounded man is the despoiled Man of Light, set upon by the Archons. The Samaritan is Simon Magus, the redeemer of the sparks of light, something for which Judaism with its pantomime rituals is incapable.

Wetbacks Crossing the River Styx[146]

A "black sheep" among the flock of Christian doctrines is the Harrowing of Hell, the belief that in the brief interval between Good Friday and Easter Sunday (or perhaps between Easter and the Ascension) Jesus, in non-physical form, went down to Hell where he engineered a prison break. Or, better, he was like American soldiers liberating a Nazi concentration camp. He was choosy, vetting the captives, setting free only the righteous heroes of the Old Testament, from Adam on up. What, you may ask, were they doing there? They couldn't get out until Jesus had paid the last farthing for them, and now he had! Is this a New Testament doctrine? Just barely: we seem to have a reference to it in Ephesians 4:8–10: "Therefore it is said, *'When he ascended on high he led a host of captives*, and he gave gifts to men.' In saying, 'He ascended,' what does it mean but that he had also *de*scended into the lower parts of the earth? He who descended is he who also ascended far above all the heavens, that he might fill all things." Though it sounds bizarre, the "harrowing" interpretation seems to fit best.

A second passage often cited in this connection is 1 Peter 4:6: "For this is why the gospel was preached even to the dead, that, though judged in the flesh like men, they might live in the spirit like God." But this looks like a "harrowing" text mostly if you think it is a follow-up to 3:18b–20a, "For Christ also died for sins once for all, the righteous for the unrighteous, that he might bring us to God, being put to death in the flesh but made alive in the spirit; *in which he went and preached to the spirits in prison, who formerly did not obey, when God's patience waited in the days of Noah,* during the building of the ark, in which a few, that is, eight per-

---

146. I must credit my old friend Charles Garofalo for this joke which has tickled me for years! Thanks, Chuck!

sons, were saved through water." But this is almost certainly based on a strategic mistranscription. The Greek of the phrase translated here as "in which also" (*en o kai*) should instead be rendered *enokai*, "Enoch"![147] Remember, ancient Greek texts had no spaces between words. So the intended reference is to 1 Enoch in which the ascended patriarch went to Sheol to give the bad news to the fallen Sons of God (Gen. 6:1–4) whose sin had caused the corruption of the human race, provoking the Flood of Noah. No reprieve for them!

To hear the whole story, we must go outside the canon. Ascension of Isaiah 9:16–18 tells, quite succinctly, of the Harrowing of Hell.

> And when He hath plundered the angel of death, He will ascend on the third day, [and he will remain in that world five hundred and forty-five days]. And then many of the righteous will ascend with Him, whose spirits do not receive their garments till the Lord Christ ascend and they ascend with Him. Then indeed they will receive their [garments and] thrones and crowns, when He has ascended into the seventh heaven."

The Gospel of Nicodemus chapters 2–10 provide a much fuller account.

> O Lord Jesus Christ, the resurrection and the life of the world, grant us grace that we may give an account of Thy resurrection, and Thy miracles which Thou didst in Hades. We then were in Hades, with all who had fallen asleep since the beginning of the world. And at the hour of midnight there rose a light as if of the sun, and shone into these dark *regions;* and we were all lighted up, and saw each other. And straightway our father Abraham was united with the patriarchs and the prophets, and at the same time they were filled with joy, and said to each other: This light is from a great source of light. The prophet Hesaias, who

---

147. J. Rendel Harris as discussed in J.N.D. Kelly, *Peter and Jude*. Harper's New Testament Commentaries (New York: Harper & Row, 1969), p. 152.

was there present, said: This light is from the Father, and from the Son, and from the Holy Spirit; about whom I prophesied when yet alive, saying, The land of Zabulon, and the land of Nephthalim, the people that sat in darkness, have seen a great light.

Then there came into the midst another, an ascetic from the desert; and the patriarchs said to him: Who art thou? And he said: I am John, the last of the prophets, who made the paths of the Son of God straight, and proclaimed to the people repentance for the remission of sins. And the Son of God came to me; and I, seeing Him a long way off, said to the people: Behold the Lamb of God, who taketh away the sin of the world. And with my hand I baptized Him in the river Jordan, and I saw like a dove also the Holy Spirit coming upon Him; and I heard also the voice of God, even the Father, thus saying: This is my beloved Son, in whom I am well pleased. And on this account He sent me also to you, to proclaim how the only begotten Son of God is coming here, that whosoever shall believe in Him shall be saved, and whosoever shall not believe in Him shall be condemned. On this account I say to you all, in order that when you see Him you all may adore Him, that now only is for you the time of repentance for having adored idols in the vain upper world, and for the sins you have committed, and that this is impossible at any other time.

While John, therefore, was thus teaching those in Hades, the first created and forefather Adam heard, and said to his son Seth: My son, I wish thee to tell the forefathers of the race of men and the prophets where I sent thee, when it fell to my lot to die. And Seth said: Prophets and patriarchs, hear. When my father Adam, the first created, was about to fall once upon a time into death, he sent me to make entreaty to God very close by the gate of paradise, that He would guide me by an angel to the tree of compassion and that I might take oil and anoint my father, and that he might rise up from his sickness: which thing, therefore, I also did. And after the prayer an angel of the Lord came, and said to me: What, Seth, dost thou ask? Dost thou ask oil which raiseth up the sick, or the tree from which this oil flows, on account of the sickness of thy father? This is not to be found now. Go, therefore, and tell thy father, that after the accomplishing of five thousand five hundred years from the creation of the world, there shall come into the earth the only begotten Son of God, being made man; and He shall anoint him with this oil, and shall raise him up; and shall wash clean, with water and with the Holy Spirit, both him and those out of him, and then shall he be healed of every disease; but now this is impossible.

When the patriarchs and the prophets heard these words, they rejoiced greatly. And when all were in such joy, came Satan the heir of darkness, and said to Hades: O all-devouring and insatiable, hear my words. There is of the race of the Jews one named Jesus, calling himself the Son of God; and being a man, by our working with them the Jews have crucified him: and now when he is dead, be ready that we may secure him here. For I know that he is a man, and I heard him also saying, My soul is exceeding sorrowful, even unto death. He has also done me many evils when living with mortals in the upper world. For wherever he found my servants, he persecuted them; and whatever men I made crooked, blind, lame, lepers, or any such thing, by a single word he healed them; and many whom I had got ready to be buried, even these through a single word he brought to life again.

Hades says: And is this man so powerful as to do such things by a single word? or if he be so, canst thou withstand him? It seems to me that, if he be so, no one will be able to withstand him. And if thou sayest that thou didst hear him dreading death, he said this mocking thee, and laughing, wishing to seize thee with the strong hand; and woe, woe to thee, to all eternity!

Satan says: O all-devouring and insatiable Hades, art thou so afraid at hearing of our common enemy? I was not afraid of him, but worked in the Jews, and they crucified him, and gave him also to drink gall with vinegar. Make ready, then, in order that you may lay fast hold of him when he comes.

Hades answered: Heir of darkness, son of destruction, devil, thou hast just now told me that many whom thou hadst made ready to be buried, be brought to life again by a single word. And if he has delivered others from the tomb, how and with what power shall he be laid hold of by us? For I not long ago swallowed down one dead, Lazarus by name; and not long after, one of the living by a single word dragged him up by force out of my bowels: and I think that it was he of whom thou speakest.

If, therefore, we receive him here, I am afraid lest perchance we be in danger even about the rest. For, lo, all those that I have swallowed from eternity I perceive to be in commotion, and I am pained in my belly. And the snatching away of Lazarus beforehand seems to me to be no good sign: for not like a dead body, but like an eagle, he flew out of me; for so suddenly did the earth throw him out. Wherefore also I adjure even thee, for thy benefit and for mine, not to bring him here; for I think that he is coming here to raise all the dead. And this I tell thee: by the darkness in which we live, if thou bring him here, not one of the dead will be left behind in it to me.

While Satan and Hades were thus speaking to each other, there was a great voice like thunder, saying: Lift up your gates, O ye rulers; and be ye lifted up, ye everlasting gates; and the King of glory shall come in. When Hades heard, he said to Satan: Go forth, if thou art able, and withstand him. Satan therefore went forth to the outside. Then Hades says to his demons: Secure well and strongly the gates of brass and the bars of iron, and attend to my bolts, and stand in order, and see to everything; for if he come in here, woe will seize us.

The forefathers having heard this, began all to revile him, saying: O all-devouring and insatiable! open, that the King of glory may come in. David the prophet says: Dost thou not know, O blind, that I when living in the world prophesied this saying: Lift up your gates, O ye rulers? Hesaias said: I, foreseeing this by the Holy Spirit, wrote: The dead shall rise up, and those in their tombs shall be raised, and those in the earth shall rejoice. And where, O death, is thy sting? where, O Hades, is thy victory?

There came, then, again a voice saying: Lift up the gates. Hades, hearing the voice the second time, answered as if forsooth he did not know, and says: Who is this King of glory? The angels of the Lord say: The Lord strong and mighty, the Lord mighty in battle. And immediately with these words the brazen gates were shattered, and the iron bars broken, and all the dead who had been bound came out of the prisons, and we with them. And the King of glory came in in the form of a man, and all the dark places of Hades were lighted up.

Immediately Hades cried out: We have been conquered: woe to us! But who art thou, that hast such power and might?

and what art thou, who comest here without sin who art seen to be small and yet of great power, lowly and exalted, the slave and the master, the soldier and the king, who hast power over the dead and the living? Thou wast nailed on the cross, and placed in the tomb; and now thou art free, and hast destroyed all our power. Art thou then the Jesus about whom the chief satrap Satan told us, that through cross and death thou art to inherit the whole world?

Then the King of glory seized the chief satrap Satan by the head, and delivered him to His angels, and said: With iron chains bind his hands and his feet, and his neck, and his mouth. Then He delivered him to Hades, and said: Take him, and keep him secure till my second appearing.

And Hades receiving Satan, said to him: Beelzebul, heir of fire and punishment, enemy of the saints, through what necessity didst thou bring about that the King of glory should be crucified, so that he should come here and deprive us *of our power?* Turn and see that not one of the dead has been left in me, but all that thou hast gained through the tree of knowledge, all hast thou lost through the tree of the cross: and all thy joy has been turned into grief; and wishing to put to death the King of glory, thou hast put thyself to death. For, since I have received thee to keep thee safe, by experience shall thou learn how many evils I shall do unto thee. O arch-devil, the beginning of death, root of sin, end of all evil, what evil didst thou find in Jesus, that thou shouldst compass his destruction? how hast thou dared to do such evil? how hast thou busied thyself to bring down such a man into this darkness, through whom thou hast been deprived of all who have died from eternity?

While Hades was thus discoursing to Satan, the King of glory stretched out His right hand, and took hold of our forefather Adam, and raised him. Then turning also to the rest, He said: Come all with me, as many as have died through the tree which he touched: for, behold, I again raise you all up through the tree of the cross. Thereupon He brought them all out, and our forefather Adam seemed to be filled with joy, and said: I thank Thy majesty, O Lord, that Thou hast brought me up out of the lowest Hades. Likewise also all the prophets and the saints said: We thank Thee, O Christ, Saviour of the world, that Thou hast brought our life up out of destruction.

And after they had thus spoken, the Saviour blessed Adam with the sign of the cross on his forehead, and did this also to tire patriarchs, and prophets, and martyrs, and forefathers; and He took them, and sprang up out of Hades. And while He was going, the holy fathers accompanying Him sang praises, saying: Blessed is He that cometh in the name of the Lord: Alleluia; to Him be the glory of all the saints.

And setting out to paradise, He took hold of our forefather Adam by the hand, and delivered him, and all the just, to the archangel Michael. And as they were going into the door of paradise, there met them two old men, to whom the holy fathers said: Who are you, who have not seen death, and have not come down into Hades, but who dwell in paradise in your bodies and your souls? One of them answered, and said: I am Enoch, who was well-pleasing to God, and who was translated hither by Him; and this is Helias the Thesbite; and we are also to live until the end of the world; and then we are to be sent by God to withstand Antichrist, and to be slain by him, and after three days to rise again, and to be snatched up in clouds to meet the Lord.

While they were thus speaking, there came another lowly man, carrying also upon his shoulders a cross, to whom the holy fathers said: Who art thou, who hast the look of a robber; and what is the cross which thou bearest upon thy shoulders? He answered: I, as you say, was a robber and a thief in the world, and for these things the Jews laid hold of me, and delivered me to the death of the cross, along with our Lord Jesus Christ. While, then, He was hanging upon the cross, I, seeing the miracles that were done, believed in Him, and entreated Him, and said, Lord, when Thou shall be King, do not forget me. And immediately He said to me, Amen, amen: to-day, I say unto thee, shall thou be with me in paradise. Therefore I came to paradise carrying my cross; and finding the archangel Michael, I said to him, Our Lord Jesus, who has been crucified, has sent me here; bring me, therefore, to the gate of Eden. And the flaming sword, seeing the sign of the cross, opened to me, and I went in. Then the archangel says to me, Wait a little, for there cometh also the forefather of the race of men, Adam, with the just, that they too may come in. And now, seeing you, I came to meet you.

The saints hearing these things, all cried out with a loud voice: Great is our Lord, and great is His strength.

On one level, the Harrowing of Hell legend attempts to solve the obvious problem of what happened to the pre-Christian saints. Could they die and go to heaven before there was an atoning crucifixion or a gospel to believe in? If they could enter the Pearly Gates without confessing Jesus, why should it be required of anyone today? Okay, they *weren't* welcome in heaven without the Jesus shibboleth, so they just had to wait, oh, a thousand or so years until Jesus arrived. But on a deeper level we may wonder if the original point was to represent the return descent of the Redeemer from the Pleroma to rescue the imprisoned photons of the *pneumatikoi* from the dark world of the Demiurge. It might be understood as an elaborate allegorical narrative of Gnostic teaching, like the Hymn of the Pearl. Thus ended the Gnostic gospel behind the gospels.

7

KING MESSIAH

The canonical gospels are not eager that anyone should believe Jesus was a revolutionary would-be king, and this makes it all the more surprising to find in their pages what seem to be clear vestiges of a story about Jesus as a messianic rebel. Such an account would be a gospel behind the gospels.

The first critical scholarly treatment of the gospels and the historical Jesus was by the eighteenth-century Deist Hermann Samuel Reimarus.[148] His verdict was that Christianity began as a revolutionary, anti-Roman conspiracy. When Jesus preached the coming of the kingdom of God, there is no good reason to think he meant anything different from the refusal of the sword-bearing Zealots to bow to any king but God and believed that God helps those who help themselves to freedom. Obviously the militant Jesus movement came to naught when Jerusalem fell to Rome, or almost to naught. It got a new start by dropping all political concerns and resigning themselves to citizenship in a kingdom not of this world. But if Christians preferred to put the past behind them, they knew that others had longer memories. They feared that Rome still suspected them of continued subversion. Else why continue under the name of a crucified rebel? What do you infer

---

148. Hermann Samuel Reimarus, *Reimarus: Fragments*. Ed. Charles H. Talbert. Trans. Ralph S. Fraser. Lives of Jesus Series (Philadelphia: Fortress Press, 1970).

when you spot someone sporting a Che Guevara T-shirt? Maybe a Kiwanis member? Christians considered it sufficient to reinterpret Jesus' execution as a holy sacrifice, redeeming believers from their sins. Reimarus was pretty cynical at this point; he figured that the disappointed lieutenants of Jesus kept the movement going as a money machine, intimidating potential givers with threats of Voodoo curses (Acts 5:1–11). The money made it worth the risk.

Why believe that Jesus was an armed, anti-Roman militant? For one thing, some of his disciples bore epithets tilting in that direction. What did "Iscariot" mean?[149] There are a few viable options. It might denote "Man of Kerioth," but that is a generic prefix meaning "Village of." Like Kiriath-Arba. Again, it could very easily mean "Man of Falsehood, the False One, the Betrayer," an infamous epithet imposed retrospectively. But it might mean "the Dagger," based on the name *Sicarii*, the assassin squad of the Zealots who carried short swords up their sleeves to stab collaborators. Obviously, had Judas formerly been a member of that elite guild but later repudiated it, he should not have retained the incriminating epithet. This implies that Jesus had use for a man with these deadly skills.

The same may be said of another disciple, Simon the Zealot. This epithet might denote merely that this Simon was known for extraordinary religious zeal (as in Galatians 1:14), but would he have for this reason stood out among a band of fanatics who had abandoned home, hearth, and family to follow Jesus? Such men were no slouches; all would seem to have been "zealots" of this type. Of course, had Jesus' men all belonged to the Zealot party, the same objection would apply: what would make him stand out?[150] But no one is saying Jesus was a card-carrying member of that "fourth philosophy." There were various militant movements,

---

149. Bertil Gårtner, *Iscariot*. Trans. Victor I. Gruhn. Facet Books Biblical Series – 29 (Philadelphia: Fortress Press, 1971).

150. S.G.F. Brandon, *The Fall of Jerusalem and the Christian Church: A Study of the Effects of the Jewish Overthrow of A.D. 70 on Christianity* (London: SPCK Press, 1951), pp. 104–105.

some allies, others not. But Simon Zelotes would have been a member of both.

Another Simon, Simon Peter, also bore an intriguing epithet: "Simon Barjona" (Matt. 13:17). This might mean "Simon, son of John, or of Jonah," but there is no other known case of "Jonah" being an abbreviated version of "Johanon." However, we do know of a sect of the *Barjonim*, meaning "Terrorists" or "Extremists,"[151] who may be synonymous with the Zealots.

Two narrative scenes in the gospels are seen in a new light once we know these things. In Luke 22:35–38 we read:

> And he said to them, "When I sent you out with no purse or bag or sandals, did you lack anything?" They said, "Nothing." He said to them, "But now, let him who has a purse take it, and likewise a bag. And let him who has no sword sell his mantle and buy one. For I tell you that this scripture must be fulfilled in me, 'And he was reckoned with transgressors'; for what is written about me has its fulfillment." And they said, "Look, Lord, here are two swords." And he said to them, "It is enough."

The other occurs soon after.

> And when those who were about him saw what would follow, they said, "Lord, shall we strike with the sword?" And one of them struck the slave of the high priest and cut off his right ear. But Jesus said, "No more of this!" And he touched his ear and healed him. Then Jesus said to the chief priests and officers of the temple and elders, who had come out against him, "Have

---

151. *Oscar Cullmann, Peter: Disciple, Apostle, Martyr: A Historical and Theological Essay*. Trans. Floyd V. Filson. Living Age Books/Mentor Books (New York: World Publishing Company, 1958), pp. 21–22; Cullmann, *The State in the New Testament* (New York: Scribners, 1956), pp. 16–17; Cullmann, *Jesus and the Revolutionaries*. Trans. Gareth Putnam (New York: Harper & Row, 1970), p. 9; Robert Eisler, *The Messiah Jesus and John the Baptist According to Flavius Josephus' Recently Discovered 'Capture of Jerusalem' and Other Jewish and Christian Sources*. Trans. Alexander Haggerty Krappe (New York: Dial Press, 1931), pp. 252–253; S.G.F. Brandon, *Jesus and the Zealots: A Study of the Political Factor in Primitive Christianity* (New York: Scribners, 1967), p. 204.

you come out as against a robber, with swords and clubs? When I was with you day after day in the temple, you did not lay hands on me. But this is your hour, and the power of darkness." (Luke 22:49–53)

Each passage contains what appears to be a redactional insertion designed to preserve the story but to remove its sting. In the first, Jesus implausibly explains that, in instructing his men to make sure they're armed, he is just setting the stage in accordance with the props stipulated by the script of prophecy. In the second, Luke has inserted a humorous healing miracle whereby Jesus reverses Peter's "mistaken" assault upon one of the arresting party, as if poor dumb Pete did not understand that they were just supposed to be engaging in a charade. Bracketing these two break-flows, we have a more natural scenario according to which Jesus tells his "troops" to prepare for a battle and prevent his arrest, and the battle does begin but is doomed from the start.[152]

Another ill-camouflaged battle in the gospel story is that of the so-called Cleansing of the Temple. As we usually imagine the scene, Jesus takes one look at the modest rummage sale going on in a church basement and starts knocking over card tables, scattering chipped dinnerware and dog-eared paperbacks. But nothing like this could have happened. Mark has completely redone a scene from "tradition" (or from a suppressed gospel behind his gospel). In reality, the Court of the Gentiles, where the livestock sellers and money changers were located, would have accommodated several football fields! Mark says Jesus and his men *occupied* the Court of the Gentiles, preventing any of the Levites from bringing sacrificial vessels through the area for use at the altar (Mark 11:15–16). Jesus simply could not have done this without a large company of armed men. At the Passover season there were extra police posted all over the place—just in case something like this should happen! As we now read it, the disturbance faded into nothing as if it had been conjured by the *Star Trek* holodeck. But maybe the hypoth-

---

152. Brandon, *Fall of Jerusalem and the Christian Church*, pp. 102–103.

esized pre-Markan version developed differently. A bit later, in Mark 15:7 we meet one Barabbas, a man arrested for committing murder "in the insurrection." Uh, *what* insurrection? Perhaps the one led by Jesus in the Temple.

But this hardly comports with our beloved picture of "gentle Jesus, meek and mild," you know, the one depicted in all those Vacation Bible School posters. But there are, again, hints suggesting that behind our gospels lies buried a pre-gospel in which Jesus preached a different message. "Think not that I came to bring peace on the earth. I came not to bring peace, but a sword" (Matt. 10:34). "From the days of John the Baptist up to now, the kingdom of heaven has been advancing with violence, and violent men seize it by force" (Matt. 11:12). One can almost hear the nervous "he-h-heh-ing" of apologists who pretend that Jesus meant only that his new (Lutheran!) teaching would create strife between family members. And that it was too bad that heroes like the Baptizer had been nastily martyred, or that the "violence" was only the irresistible progress of the mighty Christian gospel. Yeah, that's the ticket! These apologists are only trying to finish the whitewashing process begun by the canonical evangelists.

That whitewashing, as scholars have long recognized, explains several puzzling things in the canonical narratives. For one thing, the gospels not only paint Jesus as a teacher of personal repentance and piety, i.e., non-political; they go so far as to make him a pro-Roman accomodationist. As Robert Eisenman[153] points out, it is a strange Jewish Messiah who endorses payment of taxes to

---

153. Robert Eisenman, *James the Brother of Jesus: The Key to Unlocking the Secrets of Early Christianity and the Dead Sea Scrolls* (New York: Viking Press, 1996), "[T]he Flavians,,,, abetted by a host of Jewish turncoats, such as Josephus and Tiberius Alexander, seem to have marketed their own version of Jewish Messianism, which, at the very least, was presented as submissive and deferential to the power of Rome and its emperors. . . . While employing the warp and woof of Jewish Messianism, this is exploited basically to produce a pro-Roman, spiritualized, Hellenistic-style mystery religion . . ." (p. 793) "turning what was basically an aggressively apocalyptic Messianism into a more benign and pacifistic one" (p. 799).

Caesar, who tells Jews to go the second mile to carry Roman soldiers' gear a mile longer than required by law, and who advocates turning the other cheek to absorb another blow, who praises a Roman centurion for faith surpassing that of any Jew. Individually, any of these data might be defensible, but look at the pattern.

The historical character of the Jewish proceedings against Jesus has attracted several repair efforts for many years. What are the High Priest and his colleagues doing in session on Passover Eve when the Torah requires them to be home? Why do they consider Jesus' claim (or anyone else's) to Messiahsip to be "blasphemy"? And so forth. One might want to make a clean break and admit the whole thing is a fiction penned by someone who just did not know how these things worked. But this is only a partial answer. Why spin such a tale? It would make sense if a non-Jewish Christian was trying to extinguish Roman hostility toward Jesus and Christianity by shifting the blame for Jesus' execution from the Roman authorities to their Jewish counterparts. The flip side of this denarius is the wholly implausible depiction of Pontius Pilate. From Philo and Josephus we know Pilate to have been an inveterate Jew-hater who took every opportunity to outrage the sensibilities of those he governed. To imagine him even being hesitant to crucify a Messianic pretender like Jesus is fully as absurd as the ultimate outcome of this trajectory, the canonization of Pilate as a saint in the Coptic Church! The tendency could hardly be clearer. Pilate is synecdoche for Rome. Rome is being absolved.

None of this originates with me, rest assured. I gladly confess I learned it from the great S.G.F. Brandon, whose *The Fall of Jerusalem and the Christian Church* surely belongs in the Higher-Critical Hall of Fame. Brandon, quite naturally, ascribes this program of apologetical revisionism to the Christians themselves, the evangelist Mark in particular. But several recent scholars,[154] advocates of the Roman Provenance theory of Christian origins, have added a new dimension to the Brandon hypothesis. What if the "sucking

---

154. James S. Valliant and Warren Fahy, *Creating Christ: How Roman Emperors Created Christianity* (Crossroad Press, 2018).

up to the Romans" business was not the invention of the Christians but rather of *Rome?*

Before the War of 66 to 73 C.E., an (uneasy) peace was sustained by the accomodationist factions of the Jews. Roman taxes, after all, were collected at the Jerusalem Temple. Sacrifices were daily offered on behalf of the Emperor. That arrangement collapsed when the Zealots killed the Quisling priests and stopped the sacrifices for Caesar. After the war, the Jewish religious leaders, the Rabbis, were relieved to return to co-existence with Rome. But it had never been the religious hierarchy who caused trouble for the Empire. It was the popular revolutionaries one had to worry about. Might it be possible to co-opt some of *them?* Some, e.g., Joseph Atwill,[155] envision the Flavian regime concocting Christianity, a pacifistic, pro-Roman pseudo-messianic cult and propagating it among naïve Jews. Embracing it, Jews could still flatter themselves as Messianists but in such a way as to cause no more trouble for Rome. But this may be going a bit too far. All one would need to posit is that the Flavian rulers located and sponsored a group of Jewish-Christians already sympathetic to such a position, much like chastised Jews who still theoretically expected the Messiah to bring the kingdom *someday* but would willingly meanwhile bide their time.[156]

Vespasian, Titus, and the Son of Man

The Little Apocalypse of Mark 13 has Jesus predicting the end of the age to transpire in the generation of his contemporaries, not centuries or millennia later, and that it would follow at once upon the destruction of the Temple. Of course, part of this predic-

---

155. Joseph Atwill, *Caesar's Messiah: The Roman Conspiracy to Invent Jesus* (Charleston: CreateSpace, 2011).

156. C.K. Barrett, *The Gospel of John and Judaism*. Franz Delitzsch Lectures (Philadelphia: Fortress Press, 1975); Abba Hillel Silver, *A History of Messianic Speculation in Israel: From the First through the Seventeenth Centuries* (Boston: Beacon Press, 1959), p. 15.

tion was fulfilled right on time! But did Jesus return at that time? Didn't he say he would? This seeming failure of dominical prophecy embarrasses both apologists and critics. Was Jesus in error? But if it was not a genuine saying of Jesus, but an after-the-fact "postdiction," why on earth would the evangelists preserve or create a grossly embarrassing failed prophecy for Jesus?

Valliant, Fahy, and Atwill make a shocking suggestion that would, however, solve the problem: they say that it wasn't supposed to be Jesus himself returning, any more than John the Baptist was a literal return of the prophet Elijah. No, readers were intended to grasp that the ominous intervention of the (Danielic) Son of Man was not a "second coming" of Jesus Christ, but, if you are willing to accept it, rather the Roman *Titus* razing the Jerusalem Temple! Have you ever noticed that, in the Little Apocalypse of Mark 13, Jesus never says he is to return? In fact, does he not warn readers to disregard fakers who claim *they* are Christ arrived at last? He *doesn't* say they are pretending to be *Jesus* Christ! And when he says people will see the sign of the Son of Man, is he not referring to Daniel chapter 7? He does not apply it to himself. Maybe we have been misreading it all along.

This bitter pill goes down more easily once you learn that not only did Josephus declare Titus' father Vespasian (who conducted the Jewish War until he handed it over to Titus to complete) as the prophesied Jewish Messiah, but that so did Rabbi Johanon ben Zakkai! And Romans Tacitus and Suetonius did, too. As scripture had said, the Messiah had come out of the East to rule the nations. Never said he was Jewish. (Similarly, seventh-century Jews were willing to ally themselves with proto-Islamic "Hagarite" Arabs to follow Umar al-Faruq as the Messiah, though he was an Arab, not a Jew.)[157] Titus inherited his father's Messianic status, so both were deemed fulfillments of Messianic prophecy.

Again, this scenario may seem completely outlandish, but it is not. Alexander the Great, having conquered Egypt, made himself

---

157. Patricia Crone and Michael Cook, *Hagarism: The Making of the Islamic World* (Cambridge: Cambridge University Press, 1977), p. 5.

palatable to his new subjects by claiming he was the son of their god, Zeus-Amun. It further strengthens the argument if we use a wider historical lens. As it happens, we have a perfectly good historical analogy that at least shows that the kind of thing Atwill, Valliant, and Fahy posit did happen back then.[158] I am thinking of the Persian reconstruction of Judaism under Ezra and Nehemiah. It looks as if these Persian agents essentially transformed the old faith of Israel into a local variant of their own religion, Zoroastrianism. Pre-Exilic Judaism knew nothing of an eschatological resurrection and Final Judgment. Its Satan was an agent of Jehovah, not his arch-enemy. There was no dispensational periodization of world history. No virgin-born cosmic Savior. After the Exile, Pharisaism (on the way to becoming "official" Judaism) exhibits all these things, which is why the Sadducees mocked the Pharisees *as* Pharisees, i.e., "Parsees," Zoroastrians.[159] For their part some rabbis considered Zoroaster the same person as Jeremiah's disciple Baruch. The Second Isaiah (Isa. 45:1–7) called Cyrus the Great "my Messiah," so why not Vespasian/Titus?

This imposition of the Persian religion upon Judaism was of course designed to reconcile the conquered with the conqueror and, which is the same thing, to assimilate the subject people into the larger empire. Valliant and Fahy make it look very likely that Christianity began the same way.

Is there any solid evidence for the wholesale Roman fabrication of Christianity as we know it? Or is it all simply an interpretive paradigm to re-construe the textual data of the New Testament (not that that's unimportant)? Valliant and Fahy lay great store by numismatic evidence, plus ancient mosaics and tombstones which copiously display the "trademark" of Vespasian and Titus (ultimately and admittedly borrowed from the earlier

---

158. Philip R. Davies, *In Search of 'Ancient Israel.'* Journal for the Study of the Old Testament Supplement Series 148 (Sheffield: Sheffield Academic Press, 1992), pp. 76–80.

159. T.W. Manson, *The Servant Messiah: A Study of the Public Ministry of Jesus* (Cambridge at the University Press, 1961), pp. 18–20.

Seleucid emperors): the design of an anchor (sometimes a trident) flanked by dolphins or with Flipper curled around the anchor haft. Why is this important? Well, at the very same time the Flavians were minting these coins, Christians widely embraced this symbol for themselves. Christian use continued long afterward, though as of the non-Flavian Constantine it was replaced by the more familiar cross. Given the impression, reinforced by movies like *The Robe* and *Demetrius and the Gladiators*, that Rome engaged in unremitting, widespread persecution of Christians, it would seem extremely unlikely for Christians to appropriate for themselves the favorite logo of their persecutors. But it would make plenty of sense for them to use the symbol of Flavianism if the latter supported their religion—having largely created it in the first place.

Jesus Himself

So much for Christianity. Now for Christology! It starts, at least in this pre-gospel, the gospel of King Jesus, at the Jordan baptism. All three Synoptics imply some version of ancient Adoptionism, the notion that Jesus was a genuine human being, no demigod, no avatar, no theophany. But, partly due to his Davidic lineage, partly to his extraordinary righteousness, he had been adopted as God's Son. That designation goes back to the Sacred Kingship of Israel and Judah. On coronation (inauguration) day, the newly crowned king would utter, "I will tell of the decree of Yahweh! He has said to me, 'You are my Son! Today I have begotten you!'" (Psalm 2:7). Henceforth, for the duration of his reign, the king served as God's vicar upon Earth.[160] Though only a few manuscripts preserve it, I feel sure Luke 3:22 originally had the divine Voice say to Jesus, "You are my beloved Son; today I have begotten you!" God is telling him he is the King of the Jews, the Messiah. Here Kingsbury's

---

160. A.R, Johnson, "Hebrew Conceptions of Kingship." In S.H. Hooke, ed., *Myth, Ritual, and Kingship: Essays on the Theory and Practice of Kingship in the Ancient Near East and in Israel* (Oxford at the Clarendon Press, 1958), pp. 214–220.

favorite Christological title applies better than any other: "God's royal Son."

John's gospel does not relate the baptism of Jesus, but it does have John the Baptist publicly announce Jesus: "Behold! The Lamb of God who takes away the sin of the world!" (John 1:29). We are used to hearing this as a prediction of the sacrificial death of Jesus, but Raymond E. Brown[161] once suggested that the saying was pre-Johannine and that it had earlier meant to characterize Jesus (or someone!) as the Messianic Ram of 1 Enoch chapter 89, a righteous warrior king who would one day eradicate sin. I would say this formula is actually equivalent to the decree of Yahweh pronounced over the dripping head of King Jesus in Luke 3:22.

You may think all this is quite alien to conventional understanding of the role and duty of Jesus Christ, but let me assure you the opposite is the case. We often read that Jesus failed to live up to the expectations of contemporary Jewish Messianic doctrine, and this much is true—but irrelevant. It is important to keep in mind that the pre-Deuteronomic version of Israelite religion was still alive and well among the common people, despite the attempts of the authorities to suppress it. Think of 2 Maccabees 12:39 when, in the aftermath of a Hasmonean victory over the pagan Seleucid forces, the Jews are collecting their fallen, and someone notices that one of these Jewish stalwarts for Jehovah is wearing protective amulets of the Semitic gods of Jamnia!

The Deuteronomic concept of the Messiah amounted to a righteous king of David's line who would throw off the Roman yoke. And what was the *pre*-Deuteronomic version? The Anointed (=Messianic) Son of God was divine in some sense. In his annual renewal of the Mandate of Heaven he would ritually reenact the creation-by-combat myth in which Yahweh had won kingship over the gods by battling the dragon Leviathan, initially getting

---

161. Raymond E. Brown, "John the Baptist in the Gospel of John" in Brown, *New Testament Essays* (Garden City: Doubleday Image Books, 1968), pp. 179–181.

devoured,[162] then bursting out to slay the slayer, from whose sundered carcass he created the world. Victorious, the costumed king would enter the Temple and (supposedly) ascend to heaven for his yearly study of the heavenly Tablets of Destiny, gaining the wisdom needed to rule wisely over the coming year. His (pantomimed) defeat atoned for the people's sins which had sapped the vitality of the land, which his resurrection renewed. Here we have a picture of an anointed king, God's Son, who overcomes the powers of evil, atones for the sins of many, resurrects, and ascends to heaven, where he sits enthroned at his Father's right hand. Such was the myth of the Sacred King (shared across the Near Eastern monarchies), which was "incarnated" ritually by the king taking the role and office of the God. Indeed this has scant resemblance to Orthodox Jewish Messianic doctrine, but that is because the Orthodox Rabbinic model has no resemblance to the earlier form of Israelite faith. Thus, while New Testament Christology is not very *Jewish*, it corresponds point-for-point to the ancient *Israelite* royal ideology. And a surprising amount of the latter still shines through from a gospel behind the gospels.

---

162. Geo Widengren, "Early Hebrew Myths and their Interpretation," in Hooke, ed., *Myth, Ritual, and Kingship*, pp. 191–194.

8

THE DIONYSIAN GOSPEL

D.M. Murdock (Acharya S)[163] has marshaled considerable evidence indicating the surprising extent to which the biblical Moses has absorbed the traits and associations of the god Dionysus. This chapter seeks to do something similar with the Jesus character. The title of the chapter is a forthright salute to Dennis R. MacDonald and his great book *The Dionysian Gospel.*[164] In it he argues that our present Gospel of John is a combination of three component narrative sources, one of which portrayed the Christian Jesus as a kind of superior competitor to the pagan Dionysus. One shade of difference between his treatment of the Jesus/Dionysus parallels and mine is that I do not see them as a form of early Christian apologetics: "anything you can do I can do better." I can't help understanding this Dionysian Christ as a syncretistic Christianization of a cognate savior deity.

From Bibulous to Biblical: One Small Step for a Man

We begin with the Hellenistic identification of Yahweh with Di-

---

163. D.M. Murdock, *Did Moses Exist? The Myth of the Israelite Lawgiver* (Ashland, OR: Stellar House Publishing, 2014).

164. Dennis R. MacDonald, *The Dionysian Gospel: The Fourth Gospel and Euripides* (Minneapolis: Fortress Press, 2017).

onysus.[165] It was an age of cosmopolitan syncretism as cultures rubbed shoulders, inevitably influencing one another. Philosophers and priests could hardly ignore the similarities between each other's deities and indeed between whole myth-patterns. It was a path to peaceful coexistence to posit that one's own favorite god was the same as one's neighbor's, just under a different alias. Attis was Adonis was Osiris was Dionysus was Bacchus was Sabazius— *was Yahweh.*[166] In this connection I always think of this verse from 2 Maccabees: "On the monthly celebration of the king's birthday, the Jews were taken, under bitter constraint, to partake of the sacrifices; and when the feast of Dionysus came, they were compelled to walk in the procession in honor of Dionysus, wearing wreaths of ivy" (2 Macc. 6:7). Somehow I have trouble picturing these frowning Jews stiffly frolicking and capering at gunpoint. Remember that the Hasmonean insurrection was in reaction to the mass Jewish embrace of Hellenistic culture and religion. People were flocking to it, and old Mattathias and his sons had reached the boiling point. It seems to me that these "compromising" Jews were not apostates, but merely "modernists" who aroused the combatative wrath of "fundamentalists." They probably reasoned that Yahweh and Dionysus were the same God anyway, so what the heck?

So I think it was not too surprising that some Christians had trouble telling the difference between Jesus and Dionysus—if there *was* one! After all, both were dying-and rising gods, divinely begotten by senior deities upon a mortal woman (Mary in one instance, Semele in the other). Besides, there were notable similarities in the sayings and deeds of the two, to which we now turn.

Water into Wine

---

165. W.O.E. Oesterley, "The Cult of Sabazios," in S.H. Hooke, *The Labyrinth: Further Studies in the Relation between Myth and Ritual in the Ancient World* (London: SPCK Press, 1935), p. 149, n. 1.

166. Some identified Yahweh with Zeus, as in the Epistle of Aristeas, a Hellenistic Jewish work of apologetics.

My Methodist grandfather, Welby Price, used to ask his Southern Baptist wife to make him some wine (which for some reason she referred to as "acid"). She was reluctant to honor his request but would finally give in when he'd remind her that Jesus had transformed water into wine at the Cana wedding (John 2:1–11).[167]

The story has an interesting pre-history. As Raymond E. Brown cogently argued, the episode really has to have begun as a piece of the "infancy gospel" tradition collected in works like the Infancy Gospel of Thomas, the Infancy Gospel of Matthew, and the Arabic Infancy Gospel. These texts abound in unintentionally humorous stories of what Gordon Fee used to call "the Divine Brat." Young Jesus can barely tolerate the thick-headedness of the mortals among whom he is to be stranded for decades. He constantly shows himself to know more than his would-be instructors, his parents, and the religious leaders—because he is a god. It fits the pattern perfectly when, despite his impatient dismissal of his mother's request for him to do something about the wine running out at a wedding reception, he comes to the rescue by creating hundreds of gallons of vintage wine. "Is that enough for you, mom?"

But that wasn't the first appearance of the story. No, not by a long shot. It is but a late mutation of a Dionysus miracle, one annually fabricated by his priests at Elis.[168] They would pour water into one chamber of a special vessel with an inner divider. Then they would tip it to pour out wine, previously concealed there. Pretty clever, no? Interestingly, some Christians in modern times have descended to the same trickery.[169] Ultimately and obviously,

---

167. Once I tried to get my students at a Free Will Baptist college out of a tight spot. Didn't the Cana story contradict the Baptist prohibition of alcohol? I explained to them that it did indeed, but that the Baptist stance made sense as a case of *rule utilitarianism*. That is, one may grant that there is nothing sinful about moderate drinking per se, yet swear off for the sake of the "weaker brethren."

168. MacDonald, *Dionysian Gospel*, p. 41ff.

169. Kurt Koch, *The Revival in Indonesia* (Grand Rapids: Kregel Publications, 1971), pp. 147–148; George W. Peters, *Indonesia Revival:*

the whole myth boils down to the natural miracle of the process of water, enriched by the elements of the earth, becoming fermented wine.

The Fan Club

In Matthew 3:12, John the Baptizer threatens the crowds with news of the imminent advent of One "whose winnowing fan is in his hand, and he shall thoroughly purge his threshing-floor, and shall gather his wheat into the garner, but the chaff he will burn with fire unquenchable." Dionysus, a grain god, was known by the epithet of "the winnowing fan holder." Yes, it is a common metaphor given the envisioned circumstance, but common to whom? Any old grain god, I should say, whether Dionysus, Osiris, or Jesus.

Divine Vine

One almost forgets that the speaker of the True Vine discourse of John chapter 15 is Jesus. It sure sounds like Dionysus, the personification of wine and grapes. But, again, my point is that there looks to have been a pre-canonical gospel in which Jesus pretty much *was* Dionysus. Let me share an interesting discussion of the issue by Zoe Butler.[170]

> Bacchus/Bacchos or Iacchus/Iacchos or Dionysus are all variant forms of the god of the vine, the names perhaps standing for different emphases in different cultures. Apologists are quick to claim that this god was never crucified and that the third century amulet depicting him crucified was copied from Christian Iconography. I think it is extremely likely that Dionysus was thought of as crucified for the following reason.
> Viticulture has always been a major factor of Italian so-

Focus on Timor (Grand Rapids: Zondervan Publishing House, 1973), p. 85. Koch believed the reports; Peters, though also an Evangelical, was skeptical.

170. E-mail to Robert M. Price.

ciety and was so during the Roman Empire. Now it happens that when vines are grown in vineyards they are fixed to stakes. The viticulturist takes hold of the vine and divides it into two branches, pulling one branch to the right and the other to the left, binding these parts to stakes. Specifically, the viticulture calls these the two arms of the vine. The left arm of the vine is bound to the left hand stake and the right arm is bound to the right hand stake. These stakes are, of course, "*stauri*" the very same word translated as "cross." The process is literally crucifixion. The vine is fixed to one stake between two others like Jesus crucified between two thieves. In a sense, the two stakes on either side of the vine carry away the arms of the vine and could be described as "thieves."

Now it seems to me that there are other correspondences.

Jesus is "the Truth" or "the true vine." There is a strong association of truth with wine in Italy. Wine shops often display the Latin motto, "*In vino veritas*,"—In wine is truth. Dionysus was associated with wine and the states it induced, one of which was the idea that people who are filled with wine "give themselves away" so that "In wine is truth" or "In Dionysus is truth" is literally true. I also wonder if Jesus was assumed to be Dionysus because of the similarity of "DION IESOUS" to Dionysus, so that perhaps people connected Dionysus with "The follower of Dionysus" that is "IESOUS." Could Jesus have been thought of as "the New Dionysus" for this reason among Roman cultists?

Grapes are, of course, pressed, trampled on and left to ferment in a dark place, a cave or tomb, whereupon the juice turns into wine and this could be seen as a kind of resurrection.

So I wonder if part of the myth around Jesus after the destruction of the Temple might have come from viticulture. And that aside, doesn't it strongly suggest that crucifixion really was part of the Dionysus myth long before Christianity, that the crucifixion of Dionysus was as old as wine?

In support of "Dionysius" MacDonald's contention that Jesus is intended as an improvement on Dionysus, there is the characterization of him as "the *true* vine," which may well denote the genuine article as opposed to Dionysus, the cheap knock-off.[171]

---

171. MacDonald, *Dionysian Gospel*, p. 84.

But, on the other hand, the designation might naturally be taken in a Platonic sense, the divine reality from which earthly vines are derived.

Pilate as Pentheus

As MacDonald shows,[172] Jesus' interview with Pontius Pilate so closely resembles that of Dionysus with King Pentheus in Euripides' *Bacchae* as to compel us to believe the former was adapted from the latter. Both are premised upon the irony that, though the arrogant official imagines himself to be lording it over an inferior who is utterly at his mercy, the truth is that his "helpless" prisoner is fully in charge and disdainful of his "captor's" bantam-like self-congratulation. Both gods, Jesus and the incognito Dionysus, fairly scoff at the officials' pretentious delusions, and the reader laughs with them, being in on the gag. "Do you not realize that I have power to release you and power to crucify you?" "You would have no power over me unless it had been given you from above." In other words, "Pilate, you're just a flunky." Pentheus is soon overcome by Dionysus' mesmeric charm and becomes a believer in him, all of it being the god's device to send him to his doom. The persecutor becomes the persecuted, finally getting torn limb from limb by the Maenads, the frenzied groupies of Dionysus. From this point in the *Bacchae*, Pentheus' fate becomes the prototype for that of Saul of Tarsus, converted and conscripted by the Jesus whom he had persecuted in order for him to learn what it's like to take it in instead of dishing it out ("I will show him how much *he* must suffer for the sake of my name!" Acts 9:16). We must wait for later Christian legend to tell us that Pilate, too, eventually converted and perished.

> And behold, when Pilate had finished his prayer, there came a voice out of the heaven, saying: All the generations and families of the nations shall count you blessed, because under you have

---

172. MacDonald, *Dionysian Gospel*, pp. 68–71.

been fulfilled all those things said about me by the prophets; and you yourself shall be seen as my witness at my second appearing, when I shall judge the twelve tribes of Israel, and those that have not owned my name. And the prefect struck off the head of Pilate; and behold, an angel of the Lord received it. And his wife Procla, seeing the angel coming and receiving his head, being filled with joy herself also, immediately gave up the ghost, and was buried along with her husband. (The End of Pilate)

I'm All in Pieces, You Can Have Your Own Choice.

Now the birth of Dionysus was on this wise. Zeus, having the husbandly fidelity of Tony Soprano, impregnated the goddess Persephone. Hera, learning of this, suspected that Zeus would send her packing and install her rival as his new queen, with Persephone's son designated Zeus' successor. So Hera sent the Titans to kill the toddler (at first named Zagreus), and they dismembered him alive. Zeus managed to salvage the unborn godling's heart and pureed it into a potion which he fed to the virgin Semele, foretelling that the son so conceived would be immortal and would bring joy to mankind by inventing wine (cf. Gen. 5:29). Hera then tricked Semele into begging Zeus to display himself in the fullness of his thunderous glory. Reluctantly, he complied, and Semele died on the spot, electrocuted by his radiating lightnings. Fast-thinking Zeus extracted the fetus and sewed him into his thigh, from which the baby, now christened "Dionysus," was subsequently born.

The cult of Dionysus habitually commemorated the death of Zagreus/Dionysus rather messily in mad orgies of violence, ripping apart live animals (as in the 1980 exploitation film *Cannibal Holocaust*), recapitulating the celebrations of the Bacchantes/Maenads, female devotees of the god. Keep in mind that Dionysus was a god of fertility, specifically of grain and grapes, just like his Egyptian and Phrygian counterparts Osiris and Sabazius. Tamer Dionysiac rituals included sacred communion meals in which worshipers shared bread and wine as the flesh and blood of the god. This is quite important because it constitutes a dead giveaway as to the origin and character of the Christian Eucharist. It has nothing whatever to do with the Jewish Passover. For one thing, it is not actually described in paschal terms in any of the three Synoptic Last Supper scenes: no roasted lamb, no bitter herbs, no nothing. It is only the secondary narrative frame in which the disciples ask Jesus where he wants them to reserve a hall for the celebration that makes the meal scene into a Seder. Luke saw this and made a token effort to Judaize the scene by making Jesus say, "I have earnestly desired to eat *this Passover* with you before I suffer" (Luke 22:14), but even he does not trouble himself to describe the meal as a Passover Seder. And it isn't. So what *is* it?

It is a banquet dedicated to the Corn King, whether you care to call him Dionysus, Osiris, Jesus, or John Barleycorn. "This bread is my body." Who would say that except the grain god? And just whose blood is wine? The grape god's, of course. As a Jewish ritual the meal would make sense only as a survival from an earlier period when some Jews (like ones mentioned in 2 Maccabees 6:7) understood Jehovah to be the secret identity of Dionysus. Otherwise, the notion of Jewish communicants devouring human flesh and blood, even metaphorically, is impossible.

Clothes Make the Man

Dionysus was, as we have seen, torn limb from limb, then resurrected. But he was not alone. Osiris got the same treatment. His jealous brother Set had him assassinated, sealing him alive into a sarcophagus (just like Boris Karloff in *The Mummy*), where he suffocated. His coffin was then set adrift on the Nile. After an exhaustive search, his sister-wives Isis and Nephthys located it, but Set managed to steal it and proceeded to cut the corpse into pieces and FedExed them all over Egypt. Isis hit the road again and finally recovered all but the penis (a bird flew away with it!). She reassembled the body, adding a (fully functional) prosthetic phallus. Finally she anointed her husband's Frankenstein-like body, restoring him to life and potency, whereupon he impregnated her with Horus, the Sun Falcon. He was Osiris' reincarnation on earth, while Osiris' risen self descended to Amente, the Afterworld of the departed. Here he assumed his reign as Judge of the living and the dead.

Given the centuries-long Egyptian domination of Palestine, it is obvious that Osiris worship was well-known to ancient Israel. One result of this was the story of Joseph, who is basically a Hebrew version of Osiris. Consider the parallels: as Osiris was betrayed by his envious brother, so was Joseph by his ten brothers, who were sick of his bragging. They dropped the insufferable brat in a pit, from whence he was sold to Midianite (or Ishmaelite) slavers. His sinister siblings dared not confess their crime to their father Jacob but instead told him the lad had been mauled to death by an animal. They had kept Joe's fancy robe, a gift from Jacob, and they shredded it and bloodied it, offering it as evidence for their story.

Back in Egypt, Joseph had demonstrated his worth and was entrusted with great responsibility by Potiphar, an Egyptian noble. But that all ended when he hotly rebuffed Mrs. Potiphar's adulterous seductions. She cried "Rape!" and off to prison the young hero went. While doing time in the Big House, Joseph made friends with two other jailbirds, both ex-servants of Pharaoh, the royal baker and cup-bearer both of whom had somehow irritated their boss. Each has a puzzling dream. Joseph tells the cup-bearer that his dream predicts his release in three days, while the baker's signifies his soon-coming execution! Both outcomes vindicate Joseph's psychic powers. Later, Pharaoh himself has nightmares which none of his experts can interpret, so the cupbearer suggests the king consult Joseph. The Hebrew seer tells Pharaoh that his dreams presage seven years of plenteous harvest, to be followed by as many lean years. He advises Pharaoh to stockpile the surplus from the first seven years to provide a cushion for the next seven. Recognizing Joseph's wisdom, Pharaoh does everything short of abdicating in Joseph's favor! Joseph is made Grand Vizier. He has become the savior of the world, thereby fulfilling a childhood premonition of his own. His captivity in the pit and afterward in prison echo Osiris' first death in the sarcophagus and second death (so to speak) of dismemberment. The ripping up of his Technicolor Dream Coat, ostensibly a vestige of his dismemberment by a wild beast, is both a metaphor and a metonym for his physical body. And his final glorification matches the resurrection triumph of Osiris.

In many ways, the Jesus story is a rewrite of the Joseph story. Traditional Christian theology explained this, putting the cart before the horse, imagining that the Joseph saga, composed of real historical events, was a "type" foreshadowing the future events of the life of Jesus. What would be the point of such a phenomenon? None that I can see. Obviously, it is a contrived attempt to avoid the obvious conclusion that the Jesus story is a new fiction retelling an earlier, well-known story. Joseph's betrayal by his ten brothers becomes Jesus' betrayal by one of his group of "brethren." Their number is twelve, equal to the final number of Jacob's sons (i.e., with little Benjy added to the original group). As with Joseph's story in which he twice exits something equivalent to a tomb (prisons were underground dungeons), Jesus is confined in Joseph of Arimathea's tomb before his resurrection. Like Joseph, Jesus' vicissitudes eventuate in salvation for the world as well as his own enthronement. Joseph's pair of fellow inmates, one of whom dies, the other being freed, are mirrored in Luke's crucifixion scene when one of the criminals crucified alongside him mocks Jesus, the other defending him. His defender even asks Jesus to remember him when he comes to power, which matches Joseph asking the freed cup-bearer to use his restored clout to advocate Joseph's case before Pharaoh.

Possibly the most interesting Joseph/Jesus parallel has to do with Joseph's brothers' rending his robe to attest, really to simulate, his mauling by wild animals. I've already traced this back to Set's dismemberment of Osiris, but it remains to compare it to Mark's invocation of Psalm 22 to comment on the crucifixion: "They *parted my garments* among them." Again, the clothing stands for the body, this time, of Jesus. It attests the hereditary connection between Dionysus/Zagreus/Osiris, Joseph, and Jesus.

Furthermore, we can place these developments in a slightly wider context. First, it is glaringly obvious that the Genesis account of Joseph was originally a brief for the supremacy of the Joseph half-tribes of Ephraim and Manasseh. It could hardly be clearer that Joseph is being exalted as *the* Prince of Israel. Not Judah, not David. The Judah-centeredness of the Hebrew Scriptures allowed the inclusion of this saga, but oblivious of its factional implications.

Up north, however, things were different. The Joseph saga certainly inspired the creation of "Messiah ben Joseph,"[173] whose existence, we are usually assured,[174] is explicitly documented only in third-century CE rabbinic sources. But David C. Mitchell has recently documented that the advent of a Josephite/Ephraimite Messiah was a venerable Jewish doctrine already some centuries before the Common Era. Not only so, but his sufferings (and eventual death in battle against the fiendish Gog and/or Armilus), recalling those of his Genesis prototype, were understood to atone for the sins of his people. This cleared the way for the Davidic Messiah to vanquish the imperialist forces of evil. Their long years of oppression were the divine chastisement for the people's sins. With the assistance of the returned Elijah, Messiah ben David would resurrect the slain Messiah ben Joseph.[175]

---

173. David C. Mitchell, *Messiah Ben Joseph* (Newton Mears, Scotland: Campbell Publications, 2021).

174. Geza Vermes, *Jesus the Jew*, p. 140; Joseph Klausner, *Jesus of Nazareth: His Life, Times, and Teaching*. Trans. Herbert Danby (New York: Menorah Publishing Company, 1925, 1979), pp. 201, 301–302.

175. So much for Bart Ehrman's oft-played trump card to banish Jesus Mythicism, his claim that Christians could not have invented a crucified Messiah Jesus since the whole notion of a dying and atoning Messiah was unheard of in pre-Christian Jewish belief. Thus no such belief would have arisen without a historical event of "Christ crucified." But it ain't so. See Bart D. Ehrman, *Did Jesus Exist? The Historical Argument for Jesus of Nazareth* (New York: Harper One, 2013), p. 164. Ehrman's

Still another mutation of the Joseph tradition can be recognized in the Hellenistic Jewish book, *Joseph and Asenath*, in which Joseph becomes the veritable Son of God.[176] This is a novel, written in Greek, though it remains extant in a large number of manuscripts in many languages. Some date it to the first century BCE or CE,[177] while others place it ca 100–110 CE.[178] It centers on Asenath, the daughter of Potiphera, priest of On (= Beth-Shemesh). In Genesis 41:45 she is given to Joseph as his bride. The book was probably written as evangelistic propaganda for Gentile readers. They are directed to follow Asenath into the Jewish fold. Though at first reluctant to marry this foreigner, she is soon convinced of Joseph's worthiness—and more. She receives a supernatural visitation.

> the morning star rose in the eastern sky ... And lo, the heaven was torn open near the morning star and an indescribable light appeared. And Asenath fell on her face upon the ashes, and there came to her a man from heaven and stood over her head; and he called to her, Asenath, And she said, Who called me? For the door of my room is shut and the tower is high: how did he get into my room? And the man called her a second time and said, Asenath, Asenath; and she said, Here am I, my lord, tell me who you are. And the man said, I am the commander of the Lord's house and chief captain of all the host of the Most High: stand up, and I will speak to you. And she looked up and saw a man like Joseph in every respect, with a robe and a crown and a royal staff. But his face was like lightning, and his eyes were like the light of the sun, and the hairs of his head like flames of fire, and his hands and his feet like iron from a fire. And Asenath looked at him, and she fell on her face at his feet

---

argument is a cousin to the apologists' argument that Christianity could not have gotten off the ground unless Jesus had actually risen from the dead.

176. Trans. D. Cook in H.F.D. Sparks, *The Apocryphal Old Testament* (Oxford: Clarendon Press, 1984).

177. Ibid., p. 469.

178. Ibid., p. 470.

in great fear and trembling. And the man said to her, Take heart, Asenath, and do not be afraid; but stand up, and I will speak to you." (XIV.1–11). . . . And the man vanished out of her sight, and Asenath saw what looked like a chariot of fire being taken up into heaven toward the east. (XVII.6)

"And how will Joseph, the son of God, regard me, for I have spoken evil of him? Where can I flee and hide myself, for he sees everything, and no secret is safe from him, because of the great light that is in him" (VI. 2–3).

"I was foolish and reckless to despise him, and I spoke evil against him and did not know that Joseph is the son of God. For who among men will ever father such beauty, and what mother will ever bear such a light?" (VI.6–7).

"he is the first-born son of God" (XXI.3).

"he is king of the whole earth, and its savior" (XXV.6).

Joseph is "a man who . . . eats the blessed bread of life, and drinks the blessed cup of immortality, and is anointed with the blessed unction of incorruption" (VIII.5).

The chief commander of the armies of Yahweh had appeared already in Joshua 5:13–15, where he appeared to Joshua. In *Joseph and Asenath*, the character seems intended as an angelic version of Joseph (analogous to Jesus as revealed on the Mount of Transfiguration). Is he, already in the Book of Joshua, supposed to be the angelic version of an earthly hero, Joshua ("Jesus") himself? If so, it is easy to see how the notion of an earthly Jesus as invisibly the first-born Son of God, just like Joseph in *Joseph and Asenath*, evolved along the same trajectory. Remember, Joshua himself was a descendant of Joseph. Some texts even make the Josephan Messiah a new Joshua, a precedent that makes sense of the appearance in the first century CE of would-be Messiahs who intrigued the crowd with promises that they would repeat famous feats of the biblical Joshua. Theudas the Magician[179] (i.e., the miracle-worker) boasted he would stop the flow of the Jordan (cf. Josh. 4:7, 18). The unnamed Egyptian Messiah[180] promised to make the walls of Jerusalem collapse (cf. Josh. chapter 6). And then you recall that "Jesus" is the Latin form of Joshua. And you might also be reminded of John 1:45.

The Mummy's Tomb

Most of the Osiris/Jesus parallels occur in the Passion narratives of the gospels. As Randel Helms explains, the resurrection of Lazarus in John chapter 11 is plainly derived from the Osiris myth, only it is not Jesus himself who plays the role of Osiris this time but rather Lazarus. "Lazarus" is a variant of "Eleazer." Whether by etymology[181] or by punning, the name appears to derive from "El-Osiris," "God Osiris." Like Osiris, obviously, Lazarus dies and rises. His sisters throw him a Welcome Back party at Bethany. "Bethany" derives from "Beth-Anu," or "House of the Sun,"[182] i.e., the Egyptian Heliopolis. Mary anoints Jesus, who raised Lazarus and is a second guest of honor at the party. This reflects the Osiris story in which the sisters Isis and Nephthys search for the body of their husband, and Isis anoints him, raising him from the dead. Though this anointing follows Lazarus' death and resurrection, it presages those of Jesus. In John 12:7, Jesus says, "Let her keep it for the day of my burial."

In Mark, an unnamed woman anoints Jesus, again in Bethany, and Jesus defends her extravagance, explaining that "she has anointed my body beforehand for burying" (Mark 14:8). Similarly, Matthew 26:12, "In pouring this ointment on my body she has

179. Josephus, *Antiquities* 20. 97–98.

180. Josephus, *Antiquities* 20.169–171; *Wars* 2.259–263

181. Randel Helms, *Gospel Fictions* (Buffalo Prometheus Books, 1989), pp. 97–100.

182. The precise equivalent of the biblical Beth-Shemesh in 1 Samuel 6:15.

done it to prepare me for burial." This is the first shoe dropping; the second falls on Easter morning: "And when the Sabbath was past, Mary Magdalene, and Mary the mother of James, and Salome, bought spices, so that they might go and anoint him" (Mark 16:1). Luke 24:1 says, "they went to the tomb, taking the spices they had prepared." I cannot help thinking that, originally, the story of the anointing followed right here. As in the Osiris/Isis/Nephthys story, the holy women found no empty tomb but rather the dead body of their Lord and did what they had set out to do: they anointed the body. And Jesus rose up. Originally the male disciples were present, and their grousing about the waste of ointment signified their cluelessness (or unbelief) that anything extraordinary would happen. Such thick-headed skepticism is a common element in miracle stories, raising the bar for the miracle.

I find entirely plausible the theory of Gerald Massey[183] that the title or epithet "the Christ," or "Anointed One," originally denoted not a Messianic, royal anointing but rather that of an Egyptian mummy, the dead Jesus-Osiris brought back to life by anointing, performed on-site in the tomb. "Jesus Christ," then, meant "the Risen Jesus."

I suggest that the case of the Dionysian/Osirian "gospel behind the gospels" is especially emblematic of the overall theme of this book. The image of the savior god suffering dismemberment, then rebirth or resurrection in a new and triumphant form is symbolic of the prior existence of Jesus narratives, groups of stories, that wound up being split up, their components distributed among later Jesus books of an entirely different flavor.

---

183. Gerald Massey, *The Historical Jesus and the Mythical Christ, or Natural Genesis and Typology of Equinoctial Christolatry* (1883; rpt. Brooklyn: A&B Books, 1992), pp. 98–99.

9

PANTHEON OF APOSTLES

If Mark 6:14–15 and 8:27–28 hint at the existence of very different Jesus factions, each identifying him with a different hero of the holy past, I believe I see a somewhat analogous situation reflected in 1 Corinthians 1:12: "I am of Paul," "I am of Apollos," "I of Cephas," "I of Christ." Of all the theories proposed to explain the list of factions in Corinth none seems to me to have taken proper account of the strange fact that, on the face of it, Christ seems to be a factional totem on the same level with the others, whom we are used to thinking of as apostles. If we did not "know" what else we think we know about all these names and the relative importance of these personages, we would have to think, reading this verse, that for the Corinthians, Christ is another like Paul, or that Paul is another like Christ. The implication would seem to be that the tradition underlying the passage made of Jesus one more itinerant Cynic-style sage of whom some Corinthians were enamored, whether through their own former acquaintance with him in Palestine, or through the testimony of Palestinian itinerants/missionaries in Corinth such as Gerd Theissen[184] and Dieter Georgi[185] envision, or the wandering of Jesus himself in these

---

184. Gerd Theissen,. *The Social Setting of Pauline Christianity: Essays on Corinth*. Trans. John H. Schutz. Eugene, OR: Wipt and Stock Publishers, 1982).

185. Dieter Georgi, *The Opponents of Paul in Second Corinthians*. Trans.

parts, a la Barbara Thiering.[186]

Of course Ferdinand Christian Baur thought something like this, namely that the Christ party was one with the Cephas Party, and that "I am of Christ" was a way of disqualifying lesser lights like Apollos and Paul, who had not "known Christ after the flesh." But this strikes me as harmonizing exegesis, merely an attempt to shorten the list and make easier the task of explaining it. (Nonetheless, Baur's delineation of Jewish versus Hellenistic Christian parties, as far as it goes, remains quite persuasive.[187]) It seems to me, rather, that if one took his stand for Cephas, and Cephas represented the Torah-party of early Christianity, the Christ totem would be superfluous, since on any traditional picture of Christian origins, *all* would have claimed Christ with equal urgency in addition to their favorite apostle.

No, the placing of Christ alongside the others on the same shelf seems to demand something more. It would mean that this Christ would not yet have attained theological superiority over the others, who would thus not yet have been understood as merely his lieutenants, his representatives, his vicars on earth. Christ, Paul, Apollos, and Cephas must have been parallel and equivalent teachers (or saviors!). It would have been only once Christ triumphed to supersede the others that the latter would have maintained what position they could by clinging to his coattails (just as the originally independent John the Baptist hitched a ride on the Christian express by virtue of having been co-opted by Christian propaganda).

I am envisioning, albeit dimly, in a glass darkly, a stage in which Cephas (if he is indeed the same as Peter) was the rock in his own

---

Harold Attridge, Isabel and Thomas Best, Bernadette Brooten, Ron Cameron, Frank Fallon, Stephen Gero, Renate Rose, Herman Waetjen, Michael Williams (Philadelphia: Fortress Press, 1986).

186. Barbara Thiering, *Jesus & the Riddle of the Dead Sea Scrolls: Unlocking the Secrets of His Life Story* (San Francisco: HarperOne, 1992).

187. F.C. Baur, *Paul the Apostle of Jesus Christ: His Life and Work. His Epistles and His Doctrine.* Trans. A. Menzies (London and Edinburgh: Williams & Norgate, 1875), 2 vols.

right, for does not 1 Corinthians 3:11 rightly assert that "foundation stone" language cannot properly, logically, be employed in the case of a secondary figure? It would have been a stage before Luke, in his personae of Prisca and Aquila, retroactively co-opted the Alexandrian allegorist Apollos as a Christian (Acts 18:24–28), a stage in which (dare one utter it?) Apollos would perhaps have been known as Apollonius of Tyana. In this conjectural pre-dawn hour of Christianity, perhaps (as Hugh J. Schonfield thought[188]) Paul of Tarsus deemed himself set apart from his mother's womb to be the Jewish Messiah.

We might invoke the analogy of the Hebrew pantheon before Josiah, containing Yahweh, yes, but alongside him Asherah, Nehushtan/Leviathan, Shahar, Shalman, Zedek, Sakkuth, Kaiwan, Tammuz, Ishtar Shalmith, etc. It was only once Yahweh's priests cornered the market that the others were demoted or interdicted, their priests forced to accept a reduction in grade to mere Levites, Korahites, etc. Again, one thinks of Samson, Elijah, Esau, Isaac, Moses, Enoch, all sun gods eventually demoted to the stature of human patriarchs, heroes, and judges in the interests of later monotheism. Or Joshua son of the Fish, Gad, Jubal, and others, who lost their original divine standing in the wake of triumphant Yahwism. In precisely the same way, once Jesus Christ triumphed, the former adherents of saviors Paul, Apollos, and Cephas would have sought refuge, their own sects failing through attrition, with their successful competitors.

This, after all, is the very same sort of sectarian merging we can behold between the strata of a document like the Nag Hammadi *Melchizedek*[189] where the evidence is plain that a group of non-Gnostic Melchizedekians (fossils, along with the Sethian

---

188. Hugh J. Schonfield, *The Jew of Tarsus: An Unorthodox Portrait of Paul* (London: MacDonald & Co., 1946), p. 80.

189. The collection of early Gnostic manuscripts dating from the 4th century, discovered in 1945 and known as the Nag Hammadi Library, contains a tractate pertaining to Melchizedek. Here it is proposed that Melchizedek *is* Jesus Christ.

religion, of an unsuspected phylum of off-brand Judaisms) had joined forces with a more successful body of Gnostic Melchizedekians and modified their cherished scripture accordingly, finally joining with Christians on the rationale that their Jesus might as well have been the same heavenly revealer as Melchizedek. When your own sect fails, where else do you have to go? You choose the closest remaining alternative and start harmonizing your original beliefs with the new ones.

So we might be able to explain the four-fold confession of the Corinthians as a remnant of strife between adherents of four different gurus, all on a par. This would mean that the much-discussed process of Christological evolution "from Jewish prophet to Gentile god[190]" was proceeding while Paulinism was already simultaneously developing along its own independent trajectory (as also whatever movements, lost to us, Cephas and Apollo represented). And eventually Paulinism (a form of Gnosticism?) succumbed to its more successful rival faith, Christianity. In that event, the chiding voice of Paul in 1 Corinthians, redirecting Corinthian adoration away from himself and to Jesus Christ, would be of a piece with John the Baptist in the gospels, fictively pointing to Jesus as his definitive superior: "He must increase, and I must decrease" (John 2:30).

But that is not all. It would seem as well that the same sort of Christological evolution that raised Jesus from Cynic sage to Son of God[191] had been at work in the case of Paul (and other competitors, too), and that it continued on even once the rivals had capitulated to the triumphant Jesus Christ. For there are documents known to us in which the role of the various apostles (and remem-

---

190. Maurice Casey. *From Jewish Prophet to Gentile God: The Origins and Development of New Testament Christology.* (Louisville: Westminster John Knox Press, 1992).

191. Gregory A. Boyd, *Cynic Sage or Son of God? Recovering the Real Jesus in an Age of Revisionist Replies* (Eugene, OR: Wipf & Stock Publishing, 2000).

ber, as Schmithals[192] tells us, this title originally belonged not to subordinates of Jesus but to direct emissaries from the Pleroma) remains central despite superficial Christianization. In several of the Apocryphal Acts of the Apostles, it is the title character who is the real Christ. It is Paul, Peter, Thomas, John, Andrew, whose miracles cause them to be taken by their worshipful converts as gods come down to earth. It is Paul, Thomas, John, who rise from the dead, Peter who is crucified. True, as we now read them, these apostles are simply following in the footsteps of their Lord Jesus. But all the way to an empty tomb and a heavenly ascension? It is striking that in each such Acts of an apostle there sooner or later comes a scene, like clockwork, in which the reader is assured that Christ is primary, as if to correct the general impression being made, that the apostle is practically a Christ in his own right. And the key feature of these scenes is the appearance of Jesus onstage, miraculously assuming the outward, physical form of Paul, Peter, Thomas, John, Andrew. Here is an amazing admission of the very point being ostensibly concealed from the reader: the apostle is on a par with Christ, might as well *be* the Christ. Jesus is inserted as a cautionary afterthought—precisely, one may add, as in the Nag Hammadi *Melchizedek*, where throughout most of the text the heavenly revealer is the mysterious Melchizedek, king of Salem and priest of El-Elyon. But suddenly Jesus appears as his latter-day avatar. This theological afterthought is simply a way óf connecting the old faith superficially with the new, retaining as much as possible of the old faith under the guise of the new. No wonder Augustine still found it necessary to remind his hearers not to regard Melchizedek as greater than Jesus! In the same way, in the Apocryphal Acts of the Apostles we can still glimpse the personality cults of the apostles, stemming from the time before Christianity had co-opted them as it had John the Baptist.

---

192. Walter Schmithals, *Paul and the Gnostics*. Trans. John E. Steely (New York: Abingdon Press, 1972).

The Cephas Cult

Let us not overlook the ancient associations of the title borne by Simon Peter or Cephas, "the Rock." Primarily it would have denoted the navel stone, the foundation stone of the world. Jewish lore held that the Jerusalem Temple's altar stone was the stopper that prevented the eruption of the primal Deep, the *Tehom*, which, at the dawn of time, Elohim had confined beneath the Earth disk. In the Flood of Noah, the waters broke forth to submerge the Earth anew. In the aftermath, after the tub drained, God promised it would never happen again, and the navel stone was the bulwark against it. Abraham, too, was designated as the Foundation Stone.

> The matter is to be compared to a king who was desiring to build; but when he was digging for the purpose of laying the foundations, he found only swamps and mire. At last he hit on a rock, when he said, 'Here I will build.' So, too, when God was about to create the world, he foresaw the sinful generation of Enosh (when man began to profane the name of the Lord), and the wicked generations of the deluge (which said unto God, 'Depart from us'), and he said, 'How shall I create the world while these generations are certain to provoke me (by their crimes and sins)?' But when he perceived that Abraham would one day arise, he said, 'Behold, I have found the *petra* on which to build and base the world.'[193]

The epithet, actually the title, was cosmic in nature, not some amusing nickname.

But does this title really fit the cowardly dullard depicted in the gospels? Not at all. Whence such a contradiction? There are two reasons for it. First, the Simon Peter character often functions in the gospels as a foil for Jesus, a device to allow "Jesus" to explain some enigmatic thing he has just said. The evangelist anticipates his readers' questions and has Peter mouth them. "Jesus" then ex-

---

193. *Yelamdenu* quoted by the *Yalkut*, *Numbers* section 766. Quoted in Solomon Schechter, *Some Aspects of Rabbinic Theology* (New York: Macmillan, 1910), p. 59.

plains. In this way the gospels' Peter is a close analog to Ananda, the Buddha's loyal but somewhat thick-headed disciple whose bright ideas are frequently corrected by his Master, again, for the sake of the reader. Or think of poor Dr. Watson, Sherlock Holmes' unimaginative sidekick, perpetually baffled at Holmes's arcane reasoning. "I say, Holmes! How did you know little Sally was the Shropshire Slasher?" "Elementary, my dear Watson . . ." Cases of this include Mark 8:32–33; 9:5–6; 10:28; Matthew 14:28–31; 17:24–27; 18:21–22; John 13:6–10.

Other times, the unflattering portrait of Peter seems polemical, aimed at discrediting his post-Jesus ecclesiastical authority (or that of those who claimed to be his successors). The disgraceful episode of his denial of Jesus to save his own skin (Mark 14:66–72) really accuses Peter of soul-damning apostasy, for which Jesus elsewhere announces there can be no forgiveness (Mark 8:38; Matt. 12:31–32; 16:32–33).[194] This was famously the stance of Marcion, who disdained the (self-proclaimed successors of the) Twelve precisely because of their seeming obtuseness re Jesus' mission to nullify Jehovah's Torah in favor of devotion to a hitherto-unknown God of love and forgiveness. They insisted on keeping one sandaled foot in Judaism, thus effectively nullifying the message of Jesus.

I think it fair to dismiss these characterizations of Peter as genuine biographical information. To accept them as factual would be like counting the *Toledoth Jeschu* as a true account of the historical Jesus. Unfortunately, there is no better information available. But there is at least another side to the story, the story told by the Cephas cult. And it is quite the story, one with several familiar echoes. Let me remind you of what I said earlier about the "trajectories" approach pioneered by Helmut Koester and James M. Robinson. Trends seen in second-century Christian documents may often be traced back to similar phenomena in the canonical

---

194. Alfred Loisy, *The Birth of the Christian Religion*. Trans. L.P. Jacks (London: George Allen & Unwin, 1948), p. 82; Weeden, *Mark: Traditions in Conflict*, p. 38: "But it is the denial of Peter that underscores the complete and utter rejection of Jesus and his messiahship by the disciples."

texts of the New Testament. If we may recognize the later developments as the fruit of the earlier seeds planted in the New Testament, the continuity should help us better to understand both. *This* was what became *that*. *That* is what developed from *this*. The perceived continuity places a new aspect on both. Accordingly, we may come to see certain features of Petrine material in Acts in a new light by looking at it in continuity with Apocryphal traditions preserved, e.g., in the Acts of Peter. I am thinking particularly of the portrayal of Peter as a miracle-working superman, including his miracle contest with his opposite number, Simon Magus.

As Tübingen scholar Eduard Zeller[195] pointed out, Acts 9:36–38 pictures Peter as a superhero, a divine man who can be summoned like a doctor making a house call to raise the dead on demand. "This is a job for Superman!"

> Now there was at Joppa a disciple named Tabitha, which means Dorcas. She was full of good works and acts of charity. In those days she fell sick and died; and when they had washed her, they laid her in an upper room. Since Lydda was near Joppa, the disciples, hearing that Peter was there, sent two men to him entreating him, "Please come to us without delay."

Needless to say, Dorcas lived happily ever after. As in the case of Jesus (to say nothing of Elijah and Elisha), a figure of whom such things can be related is not a historical character at all. But that is hardly a surprise. Pious legends are the stock-in-trade of such movements as we are examining.

There are two moments elsewhere in the canonical Acts in which characters are said to be on the verge of worshipping Almighty Peter. In Acts 3:12 Peter heals a lame beggar, and it does not go unnoticed: "And when Peter saw it he addressed the people, 'Men of Israel, why do you wonder at this, or why do you stare at us, as though by our own power or piety we had made him walk?'"

---

195. Edward Zeller, *The Contents and Origin of the Acts of the Apostles Critically Investigated.* Trans. Joseph Dare Vol. 1 (London: Williams and Norgate, 1875; rpt. Eugene: Wipf & Stock, 2007), p. 271.

Well, Pete, what did you *expect*? Similarly, Acts 10:25–26 shows the Roman centurion Cornelius, having been directed by an angel in a dream to summon Peter, is overwhelmed when Peter actually walks into the room. Peter modestly shrugs off the acclaim: "Cornelius met him and fell down at his feet and worshiped him. But Peter lifted him up, saying, 'Stand up; I too am a man.'" I hesitate to seem to read a text against its avowed meaning, but I can't help thinking of Mark 10:18: "And Jesus said to him, 'Why do you call me good? No one is good but God alone.'" What, Jesus isn't even to be called a good teacher? Or think of the Dalai Lama who, asked by a waggish reporter, "How does it feel to be God?" replied, "I'm only a Buddhist monk." *Riiiiight*. I think Monty Python got it exactly right in *The Life of Brian*: "Only the *true* Messiah denies his divinity!" It's called "the Messianic Secret," remember? If the divine man possesses all virtues, surely modesty must be one of them. So do these Acts passages hint at a papered-over belief that Simon Peter *was* a god on earth, a savior in his own right? I do not mean to say the Acts author sees it this way. He is a "Catholicizer," programmatically trying to iron out conflicts in the early Christian movements in order to create a (fictive) ideal portrait of *"the* early Church." *He* certainly *does* want to squash all talk of a divine Peter.

Acts 8:9–24 tells the, or at least *a*, tale of Simon Magus:

> But there was a man named Simon who had previously practiced magic in the city and amazed the nation of Samaria, saying that he himself was somebody great. They all gave heed to him, from the least to the greatest, saying, "This man is that power of God which is called Great." And they gave heed to him, because for a long time he had amazed them with his magic. But when they believed Philip as he preached good news about the kingdom of God and the name of Jesus Christ, they were baptized, both men and women. Even Simon himself believed, and after being baptized he continued with Philip. And seeing signs and great miracles performed, he was amazed.
>
> Now when the apostles at Jerusalem heard that Samaria

had received the word of God, they sent to them Peter and John, who came down and prayed for them that they might receive the Holy Spirit; for it had not yet fallen on any of them, but they had only been baptized in the name of the Lord Jesus. Then they laid their hands on them and they received the Holy Spirit. Now when Simon saw that the Spirit was given through the laying on of the apostles' hands, he offered them money, saying, "Give me also this power, that any one on whom I lay my hands may receive the Holy Spirit." But Peter said to him, "Your silver perish with you, because you thought you could obtain the gift of God with money! You have neither part nor lot in this matter, for your heart is not right before God. Repent therefore of this wickedness of yours, and pray to the Lord that, if possible, the intent of your heart may be forgiven you. For I see that you are in the gall of bitterness and in the bond of iniquity." And Simon answered, "Pray for me to the Lord, that nothing of what you have said may come upon me."

I am convinced that a prior version of this story did not feature Philip the Evangelist (AKA Philip the Deacon). Originally, it cast Simon Peter as the opponent of Simon Magus, and it must have depicted a contest of miracles between the two Simons, implied in the present version in the brief notice that "Philip's" miracles put Simon's "magic" feats in the shade, winning over the fickle crowds. Why has all this been altered? It is no mystery: the Acts author is determined to make clear that only apostles can impose hands to impart the Spirit to new converts. On the one hand, this is why the deacon Philip replaces the apostle Peter in the first part of the story, so we can see for ourselves that a non-apostle cannot impart the Spirit and that an apostle can succeed where a second-rater failed. On the other, it explains why the Magus is depicted as converting to Christianity, seeking apostolic recognition, and being turned down. That is, Simon has learned the lesson the author wants the reader to see, that conveying the Spirit is the exclusive prerogative of Jesus-ordained apostles. This clown therefore doesn't qualify.

But there is more to it. As the great Tübingen critics discerned, in this story Simon Magus stands for Paul. The whole thing is a parody of the Galatians 2:1–10 pow-wow at which Paul gained the endorsement of the Jerusalem Pillars in return for his pledge to collect tribute from his Gentile congregations. Put bluntly, Paul was trying to buy an apostle license, uh, just like Simon Magus— because Simon *is* Paul.

Robbing Paul to Pay Peter

If the miracle duel between Peter and Simon Magus is only implicit in the canonical Acts, it is explicit, to say the least, in the apocryphal Acts of Peter. The whole thing must derive ultimately from the show-down between Elijah and the prophets of Baal in 1 Kings 18:19ff, but Elijah's feat of calling down fire (lightning?)[196] from the sky pales in comparison with the thaumaturgical achievements of both Simons, though the latter are extravagant to the point of being ridiculous. For instance, Peter invites Simon to the showdown by sending a dog who, like Balaam's ass, speaks with a human voice. When that fails, he sends a nursing infant doing the same stunt.[197] When a young man called Nicostratus dies, Simon takes a turn trying to restore him to life, but he is able only to make the corpse's head move a bit, then *nada*. Peter, of course, succeeds in raising Nicostratus from the dead, making the Magus look pretty shabby. Simon fakes a few more healings and conjures up phony apparitions that do not help his reputation much. Finally he announces that next morning he will ascend to God in heaven. He actually manages to get aloft in full view of awe-struck crowds who are ready to believe in him (instead of Jesus), but Peter, seeing it, prays to Jesus, telling him he'd better do something fast unless he wants to start shedding converts like rats from a sinking ship. Peter suggests pulling the plug on Simon, letting him crash and break his leg in three places. And so it transpires. Simon

---

196. As Ed Suominen suggested in an e-mail to me.

197. Making a motionless statue seem to speak, as in Revelation 13:15, was a known ventriloquist trick in the ancient world. Maybe this was, too?

hobbles away to die, and the truth of Christian belief is vindicated!

If the miracle contest between Simon Peter and Simon Magus has been suppressed in Acts chapter 8:9–24, it is not altogether absent from the book. It is hiding in plain sight. Again, it was Baur and his Tübingen disciples who delineated chains of matched miracles in Acts accredited alike to Peter and Paul. It was part and parcel, they argued, of the Acts author's "Catholicizing" agenda. Acts (in common with 1 and 2 Peter and the Pastorals) presupposes factional strife between Hellenistic non-Torah Christianity, helmed by Paul, Apollos, Barnabas, Mark, Aquila, Priscilla, etc.) on the one hand and Jewish (and Judaizing) Torah-Christianity led by the Twelve, the Jerusalem Pillars, and the Heirs of Jesus. Acts tries to reconcile the factions by assimilating the two figureheads, Peter and Paul, making them mirror one another. They say and do the same things, so if you're a Paulinist you can hardly continue to jeer at Peter since he was just like Paul (at least once Acts is done with him!), and likewise with Petrine Christians and the newly-minted Petrine Paul. One big happy family! Peter heals the lame in Acts 3:1–10; 9:32–34; Paul does the same in Acts 14:8–10. Both raise someone from the dead (Paul in 20:7–12, Peter in 9:36–42). Both experience miraculous prison breaks (Peter in Acts 12:1–13; Paul in Acts 16:25–33), both heal with extraordinary means, Paul in Acts 19:11–12, Peter in Acts 5:15;[198] and both square off against malevolent sorcerers, Paul in Acts 13:4–12, Peter in 8:9–24, as we have seen. I suggest that these remarkably symmetrical miracles that now serve to put Peter and Paul on a pious par originally found their place in a long and detailed narrative of the miracle contest between Peter and Paul (Simon Magus) in Rome. Presumably Peter was the victor in that version, just as he prevails in the Acts of Peter. Again, this is to apply the "trajectory" method of Koester and Robinson: we start with a later document and find that it sheds light on an earlier one (or on the sources behind it): "Oh! I'll bet the same notion underlies so-and so passage

---

198. "We're dealing with Med*i*evalism here, Jim!"

in the New Testament!" Or, as Derrida says, you don't know what a thing really *is* until you see more iterations of it.[199]

The whole sequence would have been analogous to that in Exodus 7:8–25; 8:1–7, 16–19, in which Pharaoh's staff magicians somehow manage to duplicate every one of Moses' miracles but finally have to concede defeat when the gnat miracle stumps them. Just so, originally I think we would have read of Paul counterfeiting each of Peter's feats, but finally running dry. Perhaps it was that, while Peter managed to heal two lame men, Paul could manage only one. Or maybe Paul's raising of Eutychus was disqualified since he might not have been genuinely dead.[200] "His life is in him"—what, "again," or "still"?

One last point: whence the astonishing business about Simon Magus' abortive ascension into heaven, issuing in a divine pummeling? Of course, it is another (pro-Petrine) version of Paul's ascension to the third heaven in 2 Corinthians 12:1–10.

> I must boast; there is nothing to be gained by it, but I will go on to visions and revelations of the Lord. I know a man in Christ who fourteen years ago was caught up to the third heaven— whether in the body or out of the body I do not know, God knows. And I know that this man was caught up into Paradise—whether in the body or out of the body I do not know, God knows— and he heard things that cannot be told, which man may not utter. On behalf of this man I will boast, but on my own behalf I will not boast, except of my weaknesses. Though if I wish to boast, I shall not be a fool, for I shall be speaking the truth. But I refrain from it, so that no one may think more of me than he sees in me or hears from me. And to keep me from being too elated by the abundance of revelations, a thorn was

---

199. Jacques Derrida, "Play: From the Pharmakon to the Letter," in Derrida, *Dissemination*. Trans. Barbara Johnson (Chicago: University of Chicago Press, 1981), p. 168: "*It appears, in its essence, as* the possibility of its own most proper non-truth, of its pseudo-truth reflected in the icon, the phantasm, or the simulacrum. What is is not what it is, identical and identical to itself, unique, unless it *adds to itself* the possibility of being *repeated* as such."

200. "But I'm *not dead!*" "*You're* not foolin' anyone!"

given me in the flesh, a messenger of Satan, to harass me, to keep me from being too elated. Three times I besought the Lord about this, that it should leave me; but he said to me, "My grace is sufficient for you, for my power is made perfect in weakness." I will all the more gladly boast of my weaknesses, that the power of Christ may rest upon me. For the sake of Christ, then, I am content with weaknesses, insults, hardships, persecutions, and calamities; for when I am weak, then I am strong.

The word rendered "harass" here actually means "to beat with the fist." This brings the story awfully close to the version in the Acts of Peter with its physical injury of the pretentious Simon, causing him to plunge earthward.

Quo Vadis?

Probably the best known bit from the Apocryphal Acts of the Apostles occurs near the end of the Acts of Peter. Peter's disciples in Rome have learned that the authorities are planning to apprehend Peter and to crucify him. With difficulty, his brethren persuade Peter to flee the city, but on his way out of Rome, who should he encounter coming in the opposite direction, but *Jesus!* "Uh, where are you going, Lord?" The answer: "To Rome, to be crucified again." Peter gets the message: someone has an appointment on a cross, and if he takes it on the lam, well, *some*body's gotta do it. Jesus is shaming him into meeting his fate, and it works! Peter turns around and retraces his steps, while Jesus ascends into the sky. It is a profound and astonishing story.

But why is Peter to be crucified? Simply because he is a Christian? Or a ring leader of Christians? Not exactly. As in the other Apocryphal Acts, the eponymous apostle is being hunted down because he preaches *encratism*, the celibacy gospel popular in various quarters of second-century Christianity. Original sin was sexual intercourse. (Encratites were also apocalypticists and repudiated the family unit, so the prospect of no future humans bothered them not at all.) Peter has won numerous wealthy women to this anti-sex evangel, and their husbands are by no means pleased. Being wealthy, they have connections in the government, and they ask their powerful pals to get rid of these holy home wreckers. And that's why the apostle of each Acts winds up martyred. The issue isn't really Jesus; it's sex. Yes, these narratives in their extant form have been Christianized, but behind them lie "gospels" of apostles like Peter, not yet demoted to apostles of Jesus Christ. But what of the martyrdom by crucifixion? Isn't that a sure sign of the essential and original Christian character of these Acts? After all, Peter is not just crucified (albeit upside down, perhaps a Christian redactional change precisely in order to distinguish Peter from Jesus?), but he even makes a postmortem appearance to Peter's disciple Marcellus, who anoints Peter's body and clothes it in fine fabrics, placing him in Marcellus' own tomb a la Joseph of Arimathea.

> And Marcellus not asking leave of any, for it was not possible, when he saw that Peter had given up the ghost, took him down from the cross with his own hands and washed him in milk and wine: and cut fine seven minae of mastic, and of myrrh and aloes and Indian leaf other fifty, and perfumed (embalmed) his body and filled a coffin of marble of great price with Attic honey and laid it in his own tomb.
>
> But Peter by night appeared unto Marcellus and said: Marcellus, hast thou heard that the Lord saith: Let the dead be buried of their own dead? And when Marcellus said: Yea, Peter said to him: That, then, which thou hast spent on the dead, thou hast lost: for thou being alive hast like a dead man cared for the dead. And Marcellus awoke and told the brethren of the appearing of Peter: and he was with them that had been stablished in the faith of Christ by Peter, himself also being stablished yet more until the coming of Paul unto Rome.

Marcellus then conveys Peter's message to his brethren. And that message is that all this funerary falderal is one big waste, since the things of the flesh are useless to the spiritually minded. Why is this ending so close to that in the canonical gospels? Well, "obviously" these Christian writers are slavishly imitating the gospels, right? Could be, but I doubt it.[201] I think rather that we are seeing a genre pattern embodied in several particular writings. It is, once again, a form of the Mythic Hero Archetype. It is not visible only in Christian writings. And you understand I am positing a Petrine but pre-Christian, hence non-Christian, document.

Paul's People

Nor is it only the Apocryphal Acts which preserve the original cults of the apostles as full rivals to Christ. Certain texts among the Pauline Epistles, some having attracted occasional puzzlement but little in the way of significant elucidation, are perhaps further fossils of the theological personality cult of Paul. In what follows, I am adopting the Dutch Radical[202] paradigm, which sees the Pauline corpus as a deposit of Paulinist thought and theology drawn from many places and times, all attributed subsequently to Paul, the eponymous patron of the sect/school.

First, in 2 Corinthians chapter 3 we have a striking midrash on Exodus 34. In it a parallel is drawn between the inaugurators of two great covenants, Moses and . . . Jesus? No, though one might have expected such. In fact it is Paul who is depicted as the new Moses, unlike, e.g., the Gospel of John, where Jesus is the antitype to Moses (John 1:17; 9:28). The Transfiguration scenes of the Synoptics and 2 Peter have Jesus repeat Moses' transfiguration, but in 2 Corinthians 3 it is Paul who has the honor. Granted, 2 Corinthians 3 is not a narrative in the same way as Matthew 17:2, but the point of comparison is precisely the same: the superiority of the new, unfading glory to the old halo of Moses, long ago faded.

---

201. I think you'll agree I'm pretty good at doubting!

202. Robert M. Price, ed., *A Wave of Hyper-Criticism: The English Writings of W.C. van Manen* (Valley, WA: Tellectual Press, 2014); Hermann Detering, "The Dutch Radical Approach to the Pauline Epistles." *Journal of Higher Criticism*. Vol. 3, no. 2 (Fall 1996), pp. 163–193. https://depts. drew.edu/jhc/detering.html.

And one must ask if a comparison which implies Paul is the messenger of the New Covenant *ipso facto* implies he is on a par not only with the Jewish Moses but with the Christian Jesus as well.

But more than this, Paul has become, like Jesus, an atoning savior! First Corinthians 1:13,[203] which immediately follows the menu of factional totems we are considering, stipulates the natural implications of setting Paul on a par with Christ: it would make it permissible to picture Paul as having died an atoning, sacrificial death such as Christianity ascribes to Jesus, and from the standpoint of *Christian* Paulinism, this has become an absurdity, even a blasphemy. In the present context, where the submission of Paul to Christ is a *fait accompli*, these implications are offered as a *reductio ad absurdum*. The goal is to discourage lingering hero-worship of Paul, just as Augustine had to suppress lingering elements of Melchizedek-worship among his own parishioners.

Some might object that the rhetorical character of the questions in verse 13 eliminates the possibility that the readers might actually have held a belief that Paul was their atoning savior. The *mē* particle surely implies that the writer has moved from a disputed point to an undisputed one. He seeks from the latter to lead the readers to agree with him concerning the former. It is assumed that all Corinthians, even the most fervent Paulinists, would chuckle at the silly notion that Paul might have been crucified for them, or that they might have been baptized into his name instead of Christ's. But then, the writer says, why not recognize that it is just as ridiculous to esteem Paul (or Cephas or Apollos) so highly as to make that loyalty a false stumbling block? I grant, that is the argument in the letter as now constructed. What I mean to say instead is that the underlying personality cult of Paul might have already followed the very lines of implication sneeringly set forth by our Christian Paulinist in 1 Corinthians 1:13. Such faith in Paul's atoning suffering meets us not implicitly but explicitly in Colossians 1:24, "Now I rejoice in my sufferings for your sake, and

---

203. 1 Cor. 1:13 "Is Christ divided? Was Paul crucified for you? Or were you baptized in the name of Paul?"

in my flesh I do share on behalf of his body which is the church in filling up what is lacking in Christ's afflictions." Note the tripartite parallelism here:

1. I rejoice in my sufferings for your sake
2. in my flesh I do share [suffering] on behalf of his body
3. [for] the church, filling up what is lacking in Christ's sufferings.

My suspicion is that someone has subsequently added the plainly epexegetical phrase "which is the church," in order to soften an even more jolting statement in which "his body" meant precisely the crucified body of Jesus. But even as it presently stands in a Christian-Gnostic Paulinist text we can see with inescapable clarity how Paul's sufferings complement and fulfill those of Christ on behalf of the elect. The development here is parallel to the growth of Marian soteriology in medieval Catholicism, whereby the sorrows of the Virgin Mary were believed to atone for sin. Mary and Paul alike had their own cults of devotion. Paul's may already have formed before his cult was Christianized, or it may have continued to develop alongside Christ-soteriology once the two sects had merged.

At any rate, in view of developments like that glimpsed in Colossians 1:24, it is not hard to see what sort of sentiments called forth the warnings of 1 Corinthians 1:13. And in light of Colossians 1:24, we might ask if there is more lying behind 1 Corinthians 1:13 than meets the eye. Is it possible that the use of the rhetorical question-form assuming a negative does *not* reflect the fact that the readers can be safely expected to share the writer's view of the matter, but rather seeks to undercut any possible positive response by taking its absurdity for granted? In this case, the writer of 1 Corinthians 1:13 might well have faced a virulent personality cult of Paul, complete with atonement and baptism.

The gospels, of course, are written retrospectively, and sometimes the device of making Jesus speak the evangelist's thoughts is so overt that the narrative veil wears particularly thin. One of these places is Luke 24:44, "These are my words which I said to you *while I was still with you*, that all things which are written of me in the Law of Moses and the Prophets and the Psalms must be fulfilled." Ostensibly Jesus must be understood to mean, "when I journeyed with you, kept company with you, before recent developments." But it is patent that the real point is that Jesus is no longer present on earth, in history, and that Luke is impersonating him in order to tell the reader what Luke *wants* him to have said when he was on earth. Compare Luke 24:6, "Remember how he spoke to you while he was still in Galilee, saying ... ?" It is at the very least a mark of pseudonymous authorship when we read occasionally in the Pauline corpus the same phrase: "Do you not remember *while I was still with you* I was telling you these things?" (2 Thes. 2:5). In this case, the pseudonymous character is clear also from the anachronism of Paul referring to "traditions" inaugurated by himself (2 Thes. 2:15), much as the spurious 2 Peter refers to predictions made by Peter long ago, forgetting for the moment his literary pose (2 Pet. 3:2–4)! Or 2 Thessalonians 3:10, "*When we were with you*, we used to give you this order: If anyone will not work, neither let him eat," is plainly post-Pauline. It reflects, in context, the *Didache*'s hostility to itinerant prophets who seem to be freeloading off the churches. It quotes oral tradition stemming from Paul!

Similarly, 2 Corinthians 11:9, "and *when I was present with you* and was in need, I was not a burden to anyone; for when the brethren came from Macedonia, they fully supplied my needs." As for the tone of the divine *Paulus Absconditus*, compare these words with those of the already exalted Son of Man in Matthew 25:35, "I was hungry and you gave me to eat; I was thirsty and you gave me drink; I was a stranger and you invited me in."

And if the voice of the long-absent apostle echoes thusly by means of literary license, as with Jesus in the gospels, the parallel does not end there. The gospels abound in exhortations ascribed to Jesus for the disciples to watch and pray, lest they be found wanting, sinful, or lazy at their tasks when their Lord returns (e.g., Mark 13:33–37; Matt. 25:1–13; Luke 21:34–36). The disciples are urged not to lose faith even when the Parousia becomes delayed (in the nature of the case a *vaticinium ex eventu*: *predicting* an *unanticipated* delay!), which had happened more than once already by the time these gospel texts were fabricated. Is it possible that the Pauline corpus presents us with a parallel here, too? I venture to suggest just that. Paul is often overheard planning to pop in for a visit to this congregation or that, but there is one place where we start to get an eerie sense of *deja vue*. In 2 Corinthians there is a strange wrangling over—the delay of Paul's promised return! It has somehow issued in a crisis of faith, a doubting of God's promises which, despite mortal reckoning, are always sure (2 Cor. 1:15–2:1). And then we pass on to threats of investigative judgment on that day when Paul shall make what sounds like an eschatological return! "I ask that when I am present I may not [have to] be bold with the confidence with which I propose to be courageous against some ... " (2 Cor. 10:2) " ... and we are ready to punish all disobedience, whenever your obedience is complete." (10:6). "I am afraid that *when I come again* my God may humiliate me before you, and I may mourn over many of those who have sinned in the past and not repented of the impurity, immorality and sensuality which they have practiced" (12:21). Here we catch echoes of the baleful diagnosis of the Son of God whose eyes are a flame of fire as he catalogues the sins for which his recalcitrant churches will receive judgment when he, too, comes again: "I have against you that you tolerate the woman Jezebel ... [who] leads my bondservants astray, so that they commit immorality and eat things sacrificed to idols. And I gave her time to repent; and she does not" (Rev. 2:20–21).

And as for Paul's fears of being "humiliated" upon his Parousia in Corinth, here we must think of the chagrin anticipated for the Son of Man who will turn away from many in shame when he returns (Mark 8:38): "Of him will the son of man be ashamed."

"This is the third time *I am coming* to you . . . I have previously said when present the second time, and though now absent I say in advance to those who have sinned in the past and to all the rest as well, that if I come again, *I will not spare*" (2 Cor. 13:1–2). One recalls here the same tones sounding forth from Revelation 21:12, "Behold, *I am coming* quickly, and my reward is with me, to render to every man as his work is." Compare Amos 1:6, "For three transgressions of Gaza, and for four, *I will not relent!* . . . I will turn my hand against Ekron; and the remnant of the Philistines shall perish!"

In the meantime, Paul is represented among his communities by the circulation of "lost," pseudonymous epistles, whose writers thus function in a manner analogous to the *Bab*s (gates) of the Hidden Imams of the Shi'ites, spokesmen providing inspired guidance to the faithful in the name of the apostle of God upon whose revelation they wait.

But that is not all Paul is pictured as doing in the time until his Parousia. In the meantime he is a lively power for swift judgment among the brethren. In Matthew's Manual of Discipline section, chapters 18–19 of his gospel, we have a procedure for judgment among the Matthean sectaries (18:15–20), culminating in the solemn act of excommunication:

> Let him be to you as a Gentile and a publican. Amen, I say to you, whatever binding decision you render on earth shall have been confirmed in heaven. . . . Again I say to you, that if two or three of you agree on earth about anything that they may ask, it shall be done for them by my Father who is in heaven. For where two or three have gathered together in my name, there am I in the midst of them.

In the corresponding section of the church manual known as 1 Corinthians we have a similar stipulation of intra-Christian arbitration, as well as the parallel measures to be taken for excommunication:

> For though absent in body I am present in spirit, and as if present, I have already pronounced judgment in the name of the Lord Jesus on the man who has done such a thing. When you are assembled, and my spirit is present, with the power of our Lord Jesus, you are to deliver this man to Satan for the destruction of the flesh, that his spirit may be saved in the day of the Lord Jesus (1 Cor. 5:3–5).

Was the historical Paul a practitioner of astral projection? Did he roam across the Dardanelles in ectoplasmic form to investigate these matters and to be present for the ceremony? Or is not this declaration exactly analogous to that made on behalf of the Risen Jesus in Matthew 18? In both cases, latter-day adherents of the Lord (whether Paul or Jesus was his name) have called down the spirit of their master from where it reclines in heavenly bliss awaiting its owner's Parousia, which judgment the particular congregational verdict anticipates.

It may seem far-fetched to suggest that Paulinists expected a second coming of the Apostle Paul, but think again of his legend as we read it in the Acts of Paul, where Paul's earthly sojourn culminates in an empty tomb and an ascension to heaven! I suggest that a second coming was by this point almost an inevitability for Pauline faith.

Finally, in light of these parallels, it is worth taking a fresh glance at 1 Corinthians 9:19–22 as possibly preserving elements of a statement of Paul's own divine incarnation. He says "For though I am free from all, I have made myself a slave to all, that I might win the more." Compare the hymn-lyric of Philippians 2:6 f., "Though he was in the form of God, ... [he] emptied himself, taking the form of a slave, being made in the likeness of men." This he did to save others, of course, as did Paul.

> "To the Jews I became as a Jew, in order to win Jews; to those under law I became as one under the law (though myself not being under the law) that I might win those under the law. To those outside the law I became as one outside the law ... that

I might win those outside the law. To the weak I became weak, that I might win the weak. I have become all things to all that I might by all means save some" (1 Cor. 9:20–22).

Here is a statement of the redeemer's docetic appearance among humanity in order to save them. He took on, not just the form of humanity (though it *is* just the outward likeness), but various different forms to save different classes of people. Remember how, in the same way, the Ascension of Isaiah 10:7–31 has Christ descend through the various heavens, at each one pausing to take on the likeness of the celestial entities living there. To the angels he became as an angel, to the Powers as a Power. In the Acts of John Jesus appears on earth in ever-changing forms. The point in all of it is to save various groups of people by matching the revealer's appearance most closely to theirs. Only lying beneath 1 Corinthians 9:19 ff is a redeemer myth starring Paul, not Jesus. What we have in this passage is no mere missionary strategy (and if we do, it is a bad one, full of hypocrisy), but rather a doctrine of polymorphous "incarnation."

Do we have any solid evidence of the belief that some revered Paul, not Jesus, as their savior? Even in 1 Corinthians 1:13 and Colossians 1:24 the Paulinist soteriology is qualified, overlaid with Christian coloring. But there is in fact one major piece of evidence in which it is Paul and not Jesus who is the redeemer of the souls of men. That is the Nag Hammadi Apocalypse of Paul. In that revelation we witness the apostle's ascent into heaven where he withstands the attack of the Demiurge's minions and is sent back to earth as the one who will redeem the elect among humanity. And in the entire text, the name of Jesus *does not appear a single time*! Paul is not said to have become the herald for Jesus' gospel of salvation, an apostle of the grace of Christ. No, it is *Paul* who is to redeem souls, in his own right. Here, I suggest, is a document produced and cherished by those who venerated Paul as the redeemer, a sect that would have abstained from any other credo than "I am of Paul."

Apostle Apollos

Permit me a bold hypothesis. In other words, I'm really going out on a limb with this one. May I invite you along for the ride?

What can we say we know about Apollos, another one of the Corinthian figureheads and, on my theory, another of the rivals of Christ in Corinth? Not much as long as we stick with 1 Corinthians. There is a bit more in Acts chapter 18, with more implied in chapter 19. The Acts author provides what appear to be conflicting data about Apollos. Did he know about Jesus or not? The phrase "he spoke and taught accurately the things concerning Jesus" would certainly seem to mean he was a Christian teacher. But immediately Acts adds, "though he knew only the baptism of John" (18:25). Darrell J. Doughty[204] reads the Acts author here as painting Apollos as some sort of pre-Christian Jewish lecturer, though prior tradition understood Apollos as already a Christian. Acts would be hiding this fact in order to downplay Apollos as an unworthy rival to Paul, to safeguard Paul's hagiographic reputation as the founder of Christianity in Corinth, since Acts has Apollos go on to Corinth in 18:27–28 before Paul gets there.

He still requires instruction from Aquila and Priscilla once he arrives from Ephesus. The couple "took him and expounded to him the way of God more accurately" (18:26). Certainly he counts as a Christian henceforth, no? Well, Acts never exactly *says* Priscilla and Aquila were Christians either! Again, they might otherwise steal Paul's glory, robbing him of the distinction of being the founder of Christianity in Ephesus. Yes, Acts does say Apollos strengthened the Corinthians by winning debates about Jesus being the Messiah, which must denote his Christian faith, but this feels like a "loose end" the Acts author neglected to snip. It wouldn't' be the first time.

After Apollos goes over to Achaia (Corinth), Paul appears in

---

204. Darrell J. Doughty, "Luke's Story of Paul in Corinth: Fictional History in Acts 18." *Journal of Higher Criticism*. Vol. 4, no. 1 (Spring, 1997), pp. 3–54.

Ephesus where he happens upon a group of ascetics. There is no visible clue to their specific affiliation, so Paul asks, "Did you receive the Holy Spirit when you believed?" (Acts 19:2). If so, then they will be fellow Christians. Their reply surprises Paul: "No, we have never even heard that there *is* a 'Holy Spirit.'" This doesn't add up. "Into what [sect], then, were you baptized?" "Into John's baptism." Okay, that would explain why they were without the Spirit, but surely disciples of John the Baptizer must have at least *heard* of the Holy Spirit, since John had predicted people will be immersed in the Spirit (Luke 3:16). These men sound quite similar to Apollos, and it seems we are to infer that these are recent converts recruited by Apollos. Like him they lack the Spirit, and they are not yet Jesus-believers.[205]

One can perhaps do a bit of harmonizing by comparing 18:25 ("he spoke and taught accurately the things concerning Jesus") with 19:4 ("John baptized with the baptism of repentance, telling the people to believe in the one who was to come after him, that is, Jesus"). It is at least plausible to suggest that Apollos' "things concerning Jesus" were tantamount to Paul's "the one who was to come, that is, Jesus." Apollos was not necessarily talking about any recent activity of a man of whom he knew, Jesus, but rather anticipating the Coming One, whom, as per the Acts author and Paul, had turned out to be Jesus.

Doughty's eagle-eye scrutiny reveals the thoroughly "Lukan"[206]

---

205. A.J. Walker, *I Am of Apollos: Light on the Synoptic Problem from a School of John the Baptist* (London: Williams & Norgate, 1931), suggests that Q was actually a pair of documents, and that the first one was compiled by Apollos and reflects the implied extent of his teaching within the limits described in Acts 18:35. He would have understood Jesus as a powerful advocate for the Baptizer, but the focus of the movement had not yet shifted to Jesus as Messiah.

206. Doughty, "Luke's Story of Paul in Corinth," p. 27. I hesitate to follow the convention of calling the Acts author "Luke" for simple convenience sake, since I favor C.C. Torrey's theory that Acts is a fusion of two documents, "1 Acts," an Aramaic text consisting of chapters 1–15, translated into Greek by the author of the sequel, "2 Acts," chapters 16–28 (see Charles Cutler Torrey, *The Composition and Date of Acts.* Harvard Theo-

character of the prose in the section now under discussion. This might be the result of the author putting his source material in his own words, but the burden of proof must be borne by the one who would maintain this (probably from an apologetical "historicizing" bias). It is simpler, that is, more economical, to regard the "Lukan"-sounding material as a free creation by the Acts author. And that puts the task of interpreting the Apollos material in a new light. It would imply that the characterization of Apollos in Acts is not necessarily a retelling of facts. So there is a reason to suggest that this portrait is a theological-polemical fiction meant to cover up and substitute for a different tradition. And what might that have been?

There is a intriguing clue in the Western text of Acts. Instead of "Apollos" we find "Apollonius," which is obviously the longer version of the same name. Nor was it a rare name, but probably the most illustrious bearer of it was the wonder-working philosopher Apollonius of Tyana. If actually a historical figure,[207] he was supposed to have shared the period of Jesus' lifetime. He was a Neo-Pythagorean itinerant sage. Is it possible that the biblical Apollos was (or was based on) none other than Apollonius of Tyana? Someone will object that Acts 18:24 makes Apollos an Alexandrian Jew, but I suspect this is part of Acts' Catholicizing agenda. If 1 Corinthians 1:12 really intends "Apollos" as Apollonius of Tyana, a Pythagorean, not a Christian, and a rival to Christ, it is hardly extraordinary to suggest that the Acts au-

logical Studies I (Cambridge: Harvard University Press, 1916). I also operate on the basis of David Trobisch's identification of the Luke-Acts redactor as Polycarp of Smyrna (see David Trobisch, *The First Edition of the New Testament* (New York: Oxford University Press, 2000); Trobisch, "Who Published the New Testament?" *Free Inquiry* 28/1 (December 2007/ January 2008), pp. 30–33. Among other things, this identification would account for the anti-Marcionite and Catholicizing character of Luke-Acts. But I am afraid that regularly referring to the Acts author as "Polycarp" might needlessly confuse readers.

207. Robert M. Price, "Was There a Historical Apollonius of Tyana?" *Journal of Higher Criticism*. Vol. 13, no. 1 (2018), pp. 4–40.

thor would attempt to paper over this disconnect by retroactively making Apollonius a Christian, as Eusebius did Philo. In fact, I would suggest that Acts has remodeled Apollonius on the Jewish philosopher and scripture exegete Philo of Alexandria. (In case you hadn't noticed, this would count as another application of the "trajectories" method: when we see what Eusebius did with Philo, we can recognize more easily what Acts was doing with Apollos "of Alexandria.")

According to Philostratus' *Life of Apollonius of Tyana*, Apollonius made a brief stopover in Corinth, but whether or not this ever actually happened, the note may possibly be a reflection of a long-standing veneration of the legended sage there.

If devotees of Christ and Apollonius were coexisting in Corinth, whether quarreling or cooperating, it would have been an ideal laboratory for syncretism, as believers in either camp borrowed symbols, ideas, and good stories from one another, whether consciously or unconsciously. It would have been quite similar to the situation obtaining among the various Mystery cults like those of Isis and Osiris, Mithras, Attis, and Eleusis. An individual might join any number of these groups at the same time. And in the Corinthian situation (which was probably not unique—why *would* it be?) we can imagine a Christ adherent recalling a juicy Apollonius tale and innocently misremembering the identity of the protagonist. I can think of four gospel stories that might have made such a transition. First, there is the story of the widow of Nain's son in Luke 7:11–17.

> He went to a city called Nain, and his disciples and a great crowd went with him. As he drew near to the gate of the city, behold, a man who had died was being carried out, the only son of his mother, and she was a widow; and a large crowd from the city was with her. And when the Lord saw her, he had compassion on her and said to her, "Do not weep." And he came and touched the bier, and the bearers stood still. And he said, "Young man, I say to you, arise." And the dead man sat up, and began to speak. And he gave him to his mother. Fear seized

them all; and they glorified God, saying, "A great prophet has arisen among us!" and "God has visited his people!" And this report concerning him spread through the whole of Judea and all the surrounding country.

Might it owe a debt to this one starring Apollonius?

Here, too, is a miracle which Apollonius worked: A girl had died just in the hour of her marriage, and the bridegroom was following her bier lamenting as was natural his marriage left unfulfilled, and the whole of Rome was mourning with him, for the maiden belonged to a consular family. Apollonius then witnessing their grief, said: 'Put down the bier, for I will stay the tears that you are shedding for this maiden.' And withal he asked what was her name. The crowd accordingly thought that he was about to deliver such an oration as is commonly delivered as much to grace the funeral as to stir up lamentation; but he did nothing of the kind, but merely touching her and whispering in secret some spell over her, at once woke up the maiden from her seeming death; and the girl spoke out loud, and returned to her father's house, just as Alcestis did when she was brought back to life by Hercules. And the relations of the maiden wanted to present him with the sum of 150, 000 sesterces, but he said he would freely present the money to the young lady by way of a dowry. Now whether he detected some spark of life in her, which those who were nursing her had not noticed,—for it is said that although it was raining at the time, a vapour went up from her face—or whether life was really extinct, and he restored it by the warmth of his touch, is a mysterious problem which neither I myself nor those who were present could decide." (4.45)[208]

Then there's Jesus' miraculous haul of fish (John 21:4–11).

Just as day was breaking, Jesus stood on the beach; yet the disciples did not know that it was Jesus. Jesus said to them, "Chil-

---

208. Conybeare trans., Loeb ed., Vol. I, pp. 457, 459.

dren, have you any fish?" They answered him, "No." He said to them, "Cast the net on the right side of the boat, and you will find some." So they cast it, and now they were not able to haul it in, for the quantity of fish. That disciple whom Jesus loved said to Peter, "It is the Lord!" When Simon Peter heard that it was the Lord, he put on his clothes, for he was stripped for work, and sprang into the sea. But the other disciples came in the boat, dragging the net full of fish, for they were not far from the land, but about a hundred yards off. When they got out on land, they saw a charcoal fire there, with fish lying on it, and bread. Jesus said to them, "Bring some of the fish that you have just caught." So Simon Peter went aboard and hauled the net ashore, full of large fish, a hundred and fifty-three of them; and although there were so many, the net was not torn.

The thing to note here is the number of fish, not to mention the absurdity of the idea that the disciples, *encountering the resurrected Son of God*—would make him wait for them to finish counting the damn fish! But all this clears up as soon as we consult what appears to be the Pythagorean original,

> At that time also, when he was journeying from Sybaris to Crotona, he met near the shore with some fishermen, who were then drawing their nets heavily laden with fishes from the deep, and told them he knew the exact number of the fish they had caught. But the fishermen promising that they would perform whatever he should order them to do, if the event corresponded with his prediction, he ordered them, after they had numbered the fish, to return them alive to the sea; and what is yet more wonderful, not one of the fish died while he stood on the shore, though they had been detained from the water a considerable time. Having therefore paid the fishermen the price of their fish, he departed for Crotona. But they everywhere divulged the fact, and having learnt his name from some children, they told it to all men. (Iamblichus, *Life of Pythagoras* 8)[209]

---

209. *Iamblichus' Life of Pythagoras*. Trans. Thomas Taylor (Rochester, VT: Inner Traditions, 1986, rpt. from 1818), p. 17.

Apollonius was, as mentioned, a Neo-Pythagorean. It would be natural for tales of Pythagoras, Apollonius' predecessor, to follow in Apollonius' train. But if Christ-sectarians borrowed it for their hero, they might have let pass a detail or two that did not neatly fit their new setting. The exact number of the fish no longer matters in the Jesus version, indeed belies it. It did matter in the Pythagorean original, where the whole point was the number: the sage "estimated" the precise count and thus won his bet. And as for that particular number, who cares? Not Christians, that's for sure, but Pythagoreans (and Neo-Pythagoreans) cared because 153 was one of their sacred triangular numbers. (You will recall that Pythagoreans held that numbers were the key to all reality.)

Luke 24:36–43 depicts Jesus' joyful post-crucifixion reunion with his stunned disciples.

> Jesus himself stood among them. But they were startled and frightened, and supposed that they saw a spirit. And he said to them, "Why are you troubled, and why do questionings rise in your hearts? See my hands and my feet, that it is I myself; handle me, and see; for a spirit has not flesh and bones as you see that I have." And while they still disbelieved for joy, and wondered, he said to them, "Have you anything here to eat?" They gave him a piece of broiled fish, and he took it and ate before them.

We usually read this as Jesus showing that he has truly risen from the dead. But maybe not. It would make sense to take the story as demonstrating that he cheated death, surviving the attempt to kill him. Had he been composed of ectoplasm ("spirit"), that would mean he *had* returned from the dead—as a ghost. Instead, he is solid flesh—still alive. His hands and feet and the fact of his eating fish all prove that he still lives, since ghosts lack tangibility and cannot eat. And that is just the point in the nearly identical scene in the *Life of Apollonius*, as follows:

> Damis' grief had just broken out afresh, and he had made some

such exclamation as the following: "Shall we ever behold, O ye gods, our noble and good companion?" when Apollonius, who had heard him—for as a matter of fact he was already present in the chamber of the nymphs—answered: "Ye shall see him, nay, ye have already seen him." "Alive?" said Demetrius, "For if you are dead, we have anyhow never ceased to lament you." Hereupon Apollonius stretched out his hand and said: "Take hold of me, and if I evade you, then I am indeed a ghost come to you from the realm of Persephone, such as the gods of the underworld reveal to those who are dejected with much mourning. But if I resist your touch, then you shall persuade Damis also that I am both alive and that I have not abandoned my body." They were no longer able to disbelieve, but rose up and threw themselves on his neck and kissed him. (Chapter XII)[210]

John 20:24–29 follows another version (John 20:19–23) of the story just discussed. Christians reading it cannot help envying the disciples who beheld Jesus on Easter. How lucky they were! Unlike us poor slobs, who have to be "satisfied" with a written story. It's like having your neighbor win the big lottery, while your ticket got you bupkis. Yeah, good for him, all right, but it's pretty lame "rejoicing." Why couldn't *you* have won that prize? The famous Doubting Thomas story is a kind of wish-fulfillment fantasy: Tom was like you, missing out, but Jesus took pity and made an encore appearance—just for him! Yeah, wouldn't that be great? But ultimately, it's just someone else to envy! It's just another damn story. I think of those awful Rapture movies popular in the 1970s. They were aimed at an audience of fundamentalists who had been constantly stimulated by apocalyptic hacks like Hal Lindsey (*The Late Great Planet Earth*) to expect the Second Coming in the very near future. These hyped-up expectations, needless to say, always fell through. But these amateurish flicks provided a "fix" for Rapture addicts. Again, one might call them "Rapture porn," a cheap thrill that's not the real thing but better than nothing. I apologize for

---

210. Trans. F.C. Conybeare, https://sacred-texts.com/cla/aot/laot/laot43.htm

the comparison, but that's the point of the Doubting Tom story, with the consolation prize of a "cold comfort" reassurance: "Have you believed because you have seen? Blessed are they who have believed without seeing." That's making virtue of necessity, getting lemons and pretending they're lemonade. "Ye are the salt in the wound."

> Now Thomas, one of the twelve, called the Twin, was not with them when Jesus came. So the other disciples told him, "We have seen the Lord." But he said to them, "Unless I see in his hands the print of the nails, and place my finger in the mark of the nails, and place my hand in his side, I will not believe." Eight days later, his disciples were again in the house, and Thomas was with them. The doors were shut, but Jesus came and stood among them, and said, "Peace be with you." Then he said to Thomas, "Put your finger here, and see my hands; and put out your hand, and place it in my side; do not be faithless, but believing." Thomas answered him, "My Lord and my God!" Jesus said to him, "Have you believed because you have seen me? Blessed are those who have not seen and yet believe."

I'm sure the same problem occurs in all religions, so there might be many Doubting Thomas stories floating around. One of them appears in the *Life of Apollonius of Tyana*.

> The young man in question . . . would on no account allow the immortality of the soul, and said, "I myself, gentlemen, have done nothing now for nine months but pray to Apollonius that he would reveal to me the truth about the soul; but he is so utterly dead that he will not appear to me in response to my entreaties, nor give me any reason to consider him immortal." Such were the young man's words on that occasion, but on the fifth day following, after discussing the same subject, he fell asleep where he was talking with them, and . . . on a sudden, like one possessed, he leaped up, still in a half sleep, streaming with perspiration, and cried out, "I believe thee!" And when those who were present asked him what was the matter; "Do you not see," said he, "Apollonius the sage, how that he is present with

us and is listening to our discussion, and is reciting wondrous verses about the soul?" "But where is he?" they asked, "For we cannot see him anywhere, although we would rather do so than possess all the blessings of mankind." And the youth replied: "It would seem that he is come to converse with myself alone concerning the tenets which I would not believe." (*Life of Apollonius of Tyana* 8:31) [211]

But, then again, this one may have originated with those who affirmed, "I am of Apollonius" in Corinth, and some Christian heard it and liked it.

To imagine the Acts author Christianizing Apollonius of Tyana is not so odd as it may seem, since even in our day some have identified Apollonius as Jesus himself,[212] while others have nominated Paul[213] as the secret identity of the sage.

---

211. Conybeare trans., Loeb ed., Vol. II. pp. 403, 404.

212. Michael Faraday, *Jesus Christ: A Fiction Founded Upon the Life of Apollonius of Tyana* (1882–3; rpt. Kessinger, 2010); Raymond W. Bernard, *The Unknown Life of Christ: Apollonius of Tyana, Who Was Replaced by Jesus of Nazareth—The Greatest Fraud in History* (CreateSpace, 2018); Jonathan Manning Roberts, *Apollonius of Tyana Identified as the Christian Jesus* (Forgotten Books, 2018); Alice Winston, *Apollonius of Tyana: The Founder of Christianity* (New York: Vintage Press, 1954).

213. R.W. Bernard, *Apollonius the Nazarene: Mystery Man of the Bible*. Vol. III, (Pomeroy: Health Research, 1956), pp. 7, 22, 33.

CONCLUSION

THE CHAPEL OF ALEXANDER SEVERUS

We are told that the third-century Emperor Alexander Severus maintained an ecumenical shrine festooned with statues of Abraham, Orpheus, Jesus, and Apollonius of Tyana.[214] It occurs to me that this image perfectly symbolizes the point of the present book: the surprising survival of vestiges of proto-Christian sects and holy narratives that were finally incorporated in our canonical New Testament and the religion(s) based on it. In Corinth there seem to have been competing factions, each backing its favorite guru. Or were Cephas, Paul, Apollos, and Christ rather more than that? I think they were. The other three must have been on a par with "Christ," or, one might say "Christs in their own right." Eventually in Corinth (and doubtless many other places) Christ, however understood and defined, dominated the field. Like John the Baptist, Paul and Cephas/Peter had to take lower positions on the Christian totem pole. But being second banana was not so bad. They continued to play the Christ role in their own superficially Christianized narratives, the Apocryphal Acts of the Apostles. They performed miracles, raised the dead, preached gospels, were martyred (some even crucified), entombed, and (some) resurrected and raptured. Sure, there were nominal references to Jesus, sometimes stale, canned, rote doctrinal packages. But you knew who was the star of the show. Even the neo-Pythagorean Apollonius

---

214. *Life of Alexander Severus, xxix.*

of Tyana was pulled into the orbit of Jesus, but he did not shine there, especially since most of his fans, like John the Baptist's (the Mandaean Gnostics), remained outside the Christian fold, at least for a good while. In an important sense, the early condition of competitive diversity returned over time in the form of Catholic worship of the saints. As Calvin quipped, most Catholics would have been surprised to learn they could pray directly to Jesus; he had become lost amid the crowd of "saintlets."

But Jesus himself was Legion, modeled upon a wide variety of old biblical figures and other mythical characters including Diony-sus, Osiris, Moses, Elijah, the Gnostic Man of Light, John the Baptist, the Sacred King, even Yahweh himself. It was a kaleidoscope of Christologies,[215] difficult but possible to detect, for instance, when we catch mentions of "another Jesus," "a different gospel." Orthodoxy could not abide such a Hall of Messianic Mirrors and got busy smashing all the images they did not like. Much was lost in this way. Fewer possibilities, fewer perspectives, were henceforth available. I think it is worth the attempt to recover them.

I am no friend of vegetables. It's one of the many aspects of my childishness. I do enjoy a minimal amount of sauce on my pizza, but that's the extent of my fraternizing with tomatoes. But I learned from shows on The Food Network about something called "heirloom tomatoes," carefully cultivated varieties that have managed to survive alongside the homogenized, generic (synthetic?) tomatoes mass-produced and sold in supermarkets. Personally, I don't eat either kind, but apparently the heirloom tomatoes are tastier than the artificial ones. I feel sure that the survival, or *revival*, of some of the suppressed species of Christianity would result in a recovery of Christianity's vitality and verve. "If the salt loses its savor, how can it be salted again?" This might do it.

---

215. Inevitably one is moved to ask, "Which one was the real Jesus?" I think we are well past that. There is no telling. It even strikes me as more plausible that these Christologies stem from disparate roots altogether, perhaps more than one based on historical individuals named "Jesus," others mythological from the ground up.

ABOUT THE AUTHOR

Robert M. Price is the host of the podcasts *The Bible Geek* and *The Human Bible*, as well as the author of many books. He is the founder and editor of the *Journal of Higher Criticism*.